BECOMING A *Money Cometh* DEMONSTRATOR

DR. LEROY THOMPSON SR.

Unless otherwise indicated, all Scripture quotations are taken from the *King James Version* of the Bible.

Becoming a Money Cometh Demonstrator

Print ISBN-13: 978-1-931804-03-5

Ebook ISBN-13: 978-1-931804-04-2

Published by Ever Increasing Word Ministries.

P.O. Box 7 Darrow, LA 70725

If you are a child of God, you are designed to become a Money Cometh demonstrator—a prophetic demonstration of the power, glory, goodness, mercy, and gracefulness of God. You are destined to be financially free and live an over-and-above lifestyle.

May you believe that, receive it, and be willing to walk it out.

— APOSTLE LEROY THOMPSON SR.

CONTENTS

INTRODUCTION

My people are destroyed for lack of knowledge...
– Hosea 4:6

I was in a financial prison for over half my life. I thought being broke and having no money made me holier. But it only made me ignorant. In 1994, God found me in a Volkswagen parked outside of a supermarket and told me *Money Cometh*. I was wild enough to believe it, and then my financial situation changed forever.

Don't close this book, remaining as ignorant as I used to be. Don't be left out of what's rightfully yours. It's time for believers to go beyond talking about God's goodness and begin to *demonstrate* just how good He truly is.

When it comes to finances in the Body of Christ, God is looking to change ignorance into intelligence. His people are destroyed for lack of knowledge.[1] His children must know they are designed to live in financial liberty—to not only sing songs and praise about His goodness but to manifest it.

God wants His children's churches, families, homes, and businesses to be financially free and off the system that the world offers. But for that to become a reality, we must give Him permission to manifest through us.

I recognize that God chose me and called me out as a financial demonstrator because my obedience and heart for His Will gave Him permission to do so. I was twenty years into my walk as a believer—having never missed a day studying His Word—when the Holy Spirit saw fit to reveal *Money Cometh* to me.

In case you're reading one of my books for the first time, you should know that I came from nothing. I'm a country boy who never paid attention in grade school and barely knew the alphabet. I grew up with an outside toilet, no air conditioning, and water that had to be pumped from a well. When I married my wife, I didn't have $100 to my name. To be honest, she married a broke sinner.

A couple years into our marriage, I was born again, and not long after, I was led into ministry and pastoral leadership. Still broke. Our church had fewer than 25 members in a small town where no cars passed by. For a long time, we were in financial distress, and the pressure was on every day.

You'd think God had made a mistake revealing *Money Cometh* to someone like me. Surely, He could have called a more esteemed individual for this prophetic word, or He could have carried it out in a larger, more important city. But He didn't. He came to an insignificant town called Darrow, Louisiana, and spoke *Money Cometh.*

From that day forward, it opened a *divine* financial flow that has never stopped. (Divine means 'of or like God'. In other words, it means no limits, no impossibilities, no measurement, and going beyond the natural realm.)

My wife and I went from the scum of the bottom—owing everybody—to now living a lifestyle overflowing with more than enough. How did we get to this wealthy place? The only explanation is that God did it. And the most important part of our story is this: He didn't do it by Himself. We worked the principles of *Money Cometh* from scratch.

Through our broke years, we kept flowing with God—tithing, sowing, and obeying His instructions. God honored it. He saw that He could trust us, even when the pressure was on, and so He took the top off!

One of the first lessons in becoming a *Money Cometh* demonstrator is learning to flow when the pressure comes on. There's a pressure that tries to make you deny that you're supposed to be in another position—a greater position. But when you choose to flow with God through it all, the pressure becomes a blessing.

There's a pressure that tries to make you deny that you're supposed to be in another position—a greater position. But when you choose to flow with God through it all, the pressure becomes a blessing.

I was buried in the Word and walking in my calling when I looked up and learned my 30-year mortgage had been paid off in only three years. Sometime later, I looked up again and my wife was telling me that I had become a multi-millionaire. I share these stories so you'll understand that what I write about isn't only what I believe is possible by faith; I *know* it's possible by manifestation.

Along with the revelation came my assignment to not only teach but also *show* God's people they don't have to be broke or living in lack anymore. For decades, this revelation has continued to be proven through my life and the lives of those connected to our ministry.

I first preached the series on *Money Cometh* in 1995. In 1996, we published the book *Money Cometh! To The Body of Christ*, which unveiled God's desire to bring large money to the Body of Christ to support the kingdom. It's been over thirty years, and I've watched it transform lives across the globe. Demonstrators have sent in letters stuffed with money, cheerfully declaring that *Money Cometh* is being fulfilled in their lives. Some have even flown in to bring their financial testimonies and seed to our headquarters.

Every visitor is a demonstration of what God said to me in the early years of ministry. He said He would "do it in Darrow", and that people would come from the North, South, East, and West. He said He would put gas in their cars, and they'd be glad to drive. He said they'd fly in and ask, "Where is Darrow?" Today, every part of this word from God has become a reality.

One man flew in from Portugal to attend our Sunday service. During his visit, he gave a written testimony to my team. In it, he said he had been sick, broke, and hurting, until one day he discovered our broadcasts online and stayed connected. His entire life changed. Today, he's no longer sick, broke, or hurting. His story is one of many. Lives and financial statuses are being changed daily, which is evidence that *Money Cometh* creates a financial flow that keeps on coming.

~

What you hold in the chapters ahead builds upon that foundation. It not only peels back more of what *Money Cometh* is and its spiritual function but also shows how you, too, can become a living demonstration of the revelation—an example others can see and follow.

I guide you through this with confidence because, as I've made known, I'm not trying to become a *Money Cometh* demonstrator by faith. I'm already walking in the manifestations of it.

The word "broke" is nowhere in my vocabulary—it has been removed from my mind, my bank account, my household, and every other area of my life. My wife and I have left everything less than God's best in the past. We are living the supernatural, abundant lifestyle that God has designed *all* Christians to live.

We are not ashamed of this gospel. We are fully supplied by God, and because of that, wealth and prosperity are all over us.

The same God who did it for us is ready to do it for you. It doesn't matter what your financial situation looks like or where you are from. If it can happen for a country boy in Darrow, it's proof that *Money Cometh* can manifest through anyone, anywhere.

Your Financial Inversion

In 1978, a minister by the name of Charles Capps, in Honolulu, HI, prophesied this:

> *"Financial inversion shall increase in these days. For you see, it is My desire to move in the realm of your financial prosperity. Release Me, saith the Lord, release Me that I may come in your behalf and move on your behalf.*
>
> *For yes, yes, there shall be in this hour financial distress here and there. The economy shall go up, and it will go down; but those that learn to walk in the Word, they shall see the prosperity of the Word come forth in this hour in a way that has not been seen by men in days past.*
>
> *Yes, there's coming a financial inversion in the world's system…"*

I believe this prophecy was spoken from Heaven for me to carry out. The word *inversion* means 'reversal of the normal order'. Therefore, this prophecy confirms that *the normal order of finances will reverse* for the children of God in these times. Believers are often stuck rehearsing normal patterns instead of reversing them. They think, *This is all that I can do.* But that's a lie they've believed too long.

Over 16 years later, *Money Cometh* was sent prophetically by God to change the normal order of finances for the Body of Christ. Through the revelation of *Money Cometh*, a child of God's normal order of finances can be reversed.

You cannot be a *Money Cometh* demonstrator living under the financial burdens you've been under. Financial inversion is available, but to experience it, it must become real on the inside of you first. The only reason any child of God is *not* living an abundant life or out of debt is because of themselves. It's not because of Satan, or the senator, or the governor, or the president.

Financial inversion is available, but it must become real on the inside of you first.

The only person who can stop your financial move is *you*.

Financial inversion is like a river behind a dam. It's just sitting there, and it's not waiting for anyone else but you to open it. But before financial inversion can flow, there must be a soul inversion within you.

— Excerpt from my book, *Money Cometh Hidden Wisdom*

Believing God's Prophet

King Jehoshaphat, the king of Judah, faced an impossible situation. In Second Chronicles 20, we read how several large armies had turned against Judah, and all odds were stacked against him.

Jehoshaphat sought the Lord and called for a fast throughout the land. Their situation reversed directions when the Spirit of the Lord came upon Jahaziel, a Levite, who prophesied a word from God:

"—Thus saith the Lord unto you, Be

> not afraid nor dismayed by
> reason of this great multitude; for
> the battle is not yours, but
> God's…
> Ye shall not need to fight in this
> battle: set yourselves, stand ye
> still, and see the salvation of the
> LORD with you, O Judah and
> Jerusalem: fear not, nor be
> dismayed; to morrow go out
> against them: for the LORD will
> be with you."
>
> — 2 CHRONICLES 20:15 & 17

After hearing the prophet Jahaziel speak what God said about their situation, the congregation fell and worshipped God. The next morning, Jehoshaphat declared:

> "Believe in the Lord your God, so
> shall ye be established; believe his
> prophets, so shall ye prosper."
>
> — 2 CHRONICLES 20:20

This is a foundational principle. Jehoshaphat is revealing that you can believe in God and still not prosper if you don't also believe the words of His prophet, the one He sent. Why is that true? Because God has designed everything to flow a certain way, and we must honor and yield to that structure.

Judah never fought that battle. As they went out before the army, the king appointed singers to praise the Lord.

When they began to sing, the Lord set an ambush, and the opposing armies turned on each other, destroying themselves. Then came their unexpected prosperous results.

The Scripture reads:

> "When Jehoshaphat and his people came to take away the spoil of them, they found among them in abundance both riches with the dead bodies, and precious jewels, which they stripped off for themselves, more than they could carry away: and they were three days in gathering of the spoil, it was so much."
>
> — 2 CHRONICLES 20:25

We can't ignore what happened here. The people of God spent three days gathering the wealth—and it was more than they could carry! This is a demonstration of abundance, wealth, increase, and more than enough.

This story teaches two things. First, it reveals how God reverses situations uniquely and out of the ordinary. We are not to expect Him to guide us into financial abundance in a way that looks like someone else's story. God writes unique testimonies to display that He can use *any* supernatural route to demonstrate. He doesn't have to operate within natural patterns by any means.

Secondly, this story reveals that many times our prosperity is in the words of a prophet that God sent to speak to us. Before Judah heard Jahaziel prophesy, their condition looked hopeless. They were outnumbered with no way out.

But when they decided to believe the words of God's prophet, their problem turned into a prosperous blessing.

When they decided to believe the words of God's prophet, their problem turned into a prosperous blessing.

Anointed prophets and apostles are foundational builders of the spirit realm. The Apostle Paul explains in Ephesians 2:20 that the children of God are being built up together "upon the foundation of the apostles and prophets, Jesus Christ himself being the chief corner stone."[2] He's referring to the foundational revelation, impartation, and instruments of the Spirit that the Father uses through the apostles and prophets. That's why the enemy fights to cut them out.

The *apostolic* ministry is about establishing the foundational government in the Body of Christ, while the *prophetic* ministry brings the Body of Christ back into alignment with God's government. Those who are appointed as apostles and prophets operate with a governmental anointing, speaking with the voice of God as they continually follow the Holy Spirit's guidance. When the children of God yield to this divine order, they position themselves to receive the manifestations that come from it.[3]

When the children of God yield to this divine order, they position themselves to receive the manifestations that come from it.

I write to you as an apostle and prophet in the name of the Lord, called by God. My ministry—with *proven* manifestations—is surrounded by prosperity and wealth because God chose it to spread the message of *Money Cometh*, apostolically and prophetically.

As Jahaziel was sent to prophesy over Judah, I was sent to prophesy *Money Cometh* over your financial drought. With no respect to what level you are at, the amount of money you bring in each month, or how much financial pressure is on you—believe and receive it and see how God turns your impossible situation into abundance.

Your eyes must be open in the realm of supernatural money and open to the fact that there are no financial impossibilities in your life.

— Excerpt from my book, *Never Go After Money*

PART I
UNDERSTANDING WHY GOD'S CHILDREN MUST DEMONSTRATE

YOUR DIVINE NATURE OF RICHNESS

You have a divine assignment from Heaven, and God desires for you to walk in prosperity with that assignment.

For too long, prosperity and wealth have been a lackadaisical matter in the Body of Christ. We've talked about it but have not *demonstrated* it.

My question for God's people is this: What have you been doing with the power you've been given? Have you only been reading about it in the Bible? Only talking about it in church?

Too many Christians are content with seeing movie stars and athletes live extravagant lives, while they only talk and sing about our great God in church—then they go home to living paycheck to paycheck and drowning in debt.

This is backwards.

These loving people of God are living ghetto lives compared to what the Father wants for them.

You might think, "I own two cars. I'm not living in

poverty." But even with two or three cars in the driveway, you are still settling for less than what God intends for you. God's children are meant to have *money-freedom* lifestyles—to be out of debt, with fourteen cars and thirteen goats, so to speak. I'm talking about an overwhelming supply.

A *money-freedom* lifestyle means you're not asking or worrying about money, ever. It goes beyond what any education could give you. It's about being called to live "the good life" supernaturally—and not to live in a constant state of hustling like the struggles of the secular world. Yet, there are ministries and believers who have fallen into this hustle trap.

Why has it come to this? The system of God's kingdom, which is His way of doing things, was sent to be an example for the world's system to adopt, not the other way around. Yet, the Church has done the opposite of being an example —she has, in many ways, taken upon the world's system. This has caused the Church to not see the necessary progress in prosperity and wealth as she should.

The system of God's kingdom, which is His way of doing things, was sent to be an example for the world's system to adopt, not the other way around.

God has spoken *Money Cometh* to the Body of Christ so that we no longer have to live sad, struggling lives. Through revelation, He has given us prophetic insight, allowing us to obtain what the Church has mostly alluded to for years. It reveals that we have no business having a problem with our finances if we are part of the Body of Christ. Why spend your entire life living from paycheck to paycheck when God is not only with you but has also given you access to His insight and wisdom?

Regardless of the government's decisions or how hard the economy slams the earth—you, a child of the living God, should be able to buy what you need, what you desire, and have enough to help someone else. Your cup runs over despite outside circumstances.[1] The only question is: are you going to believe that?

IF WE PAY ATTENTION, through the revelation of *Money Cometh*, He's putting an end to this disgrace on the Body of Christ. Personally, for years, I disgraced Him without realizing it. I didn't know He was concerned about my paycheck-to-paycheck and barely-getting-by living. Even as a Christian man, I was settling for an average life instead of the heavenly life He designed for me to access here on earth.

When we are born again, we are called by God to be blessed and financially free. We cannot afford to settle for average. Walking in abundance and overflowing in God's goodness is our divine right. We ought to demonstrate heaven on earth in every area of our lives.

God is rich, which means there's a divine nature of richness living inside you already. (Let me say that again: *God is rich.*) When you yield to that inner nature, it manifests demonstrations on the outside. And when prosperity, wealth, and increase manifest from that divine nature within you, they can never change how much you love God.

God is rich, which means there's a divine nature of richness living inside you already.

When God changed my financial status forever, the wealth never pulled me away from Him. My wife and children—the closest people to me—can testify. Since the day I was born again in 1973, I've devoted every day to the Lord in prayer and study of His Word. There is absolutely nothing money can buy that could take the place of God in my life. He has first place. And walking in your rightful place as a *Money Cometh* demonstrator means He will always have first place in your life as well.

This revelation is not about personal gain, although personal gain does come as a result. It's about the kingdom of God and His Will. As partakers, you get to enjoy the benefits of the relationship. It's not *about* you, but it's *for* you.

Your wealth and abundance are rooted in God's love for you. If you believe He loves you enough to save your soul, don't you think He loves you enough to bless you financially?

If He loves you enough to heal your body, doesn't He love you enough to cancel your debt?

God promotes you because He *loves* you. He wants you to have the best, live in total peace, and give Him the glory through it all. He's waiting for you to step into this divine design for your life and be part of the remnant.

Will You Be Part of the Remnant?

The revelation of *Money Cometh* isn't for everyone. Many Christians will miss it, never seeing or having faith for it.

Likely because they have been trained too religiously. And religion often chokes revelation. Religion has been around for so long that it has gained seniority over fresh revelation. This causes good people who love God to miss out on all that God is trying to do in their lives. As a result, there will only be a remnant of God's children who take hold of this revelation and be willing to walk it out.

The Church has largely fought against the concept of living a wealthy life, so an uprooting of this religious disturbance is necessary. We must finally let revelation take religion over.

The Holy Spirit is ready to raise up this group of believers who becomes a light of God's goodness. This remnant will understand that money is not evil and that it pleases God to make large financial moves under His instruction. They will not only recognize the examples of money-freedom lifestyles in the Bible—like Abraham, Isaac, and Jesus—but they'll also be examples themselves.

They won't just talk about what Abraham had, but they'll know that Abraham's God is *their* God. And they'll have evidence in their lives to back it up.

What It Means to Be a Money Cometh Demonstrator

The enemy doesn't want us to demonstrate in a way that makes the world take notice—seeing us wearing the best, driving the best, and living in the best, while also declaring, *Hallelujah! Praise God! Glory to God! The Lord is good, and His mercy endures forever!* Satan knows exactly what that would do, so he tries to keep God's people broke and hustling to survive financially.

However, after reading this book, you have an opportunity—through revelation and insight—to position yourself for divine financial manifestations to birth in your life. If you have a receptive heart, this anointing can rest on you.

God is looking for *Money Cometh* demonstrators who are willing to do what it takes to break free from the enemy's financial strongholds and make financial moves for the gospel. He is looking for those He can pour out His blessings upon and who will unashamedly testify about it.

Becoming a *Money Cometh* demonstrator is about growing to a place where God can genuinely trust you and show imprints in your life beyond normal living.

Those who are determined to become *Money Cometh* demonstrators are proclaiming they are ready to:

- turn their finances over to God
- be out of debt and out of the system's rat race
- be kingdom supporters and big givers who have more than enough, all the time, in every situation
- be hearers *and* doers of the Word
- be willing *and* obedient in all areas, including their finances
- no longer allow the secular world to influence or intimidate them financially

Money Cometh is not for some change in your pocket; it means complete deliverance God's way. There will be God-loving demonstrators with great wealth who restore the spreading of the gospel. They will have more than just nice houses and cars; they will clothe those who don't have clothes, feed the hungry, and give with no limits. They will have enough money to shake up whatever space God calls them to disrupt.

Money Cometh is not for some change in your pocket; it means complete deliverance God's way.

To get there, recognize that *Money Cometh* is not a man's idea. It's something supernatural that God, not a man, is doing in the earth's realm. God sent it to *you*—and you must own it for yourself with boldness. When you do, you'll demonstrate His glory in how you spend, give, and live.

BEYOND THE FLESH

Money Cometh is about more than money—it is personal attention from Heaven and a spiritual function flowing through the Holy Spirit to God's children.

Money Cometh was sent to rescue and resurrect the Body of Christ in finances, calling you to no longer be *work-conscious* but to be *Word-conscious* concerning money. It represents all that God is, all that God has, and all that God can do. It declares a better, healthier, and longer life for every son and daughter of God who wants to receive it. Through it, the stress is taken off, and the best is put on.

But understanding what *Money Cometh* was sent to do and who it is for is not enough to become a demonstrator of it; you must also understand its *spiritual* functions—revelation and anointing. It carries an anointing for outcomes in your finances that go beyond the flesh. That anointing destroys financial yokes and takes away all financial burdens.[1]

Money Cometh is not a slogan; it is supernatural language sent from Heaven. And anything sent from Heaven must operate by the Spirit. The flesh alone cannot manifest it. Therefore, to walk in the demonstrator flow of the revelation and reach financial levels you've never seen before, spiritual maturity is necessary. You'll have to make moves despite what anyone else says about it.

The divine secrets to becoming a *Money Cometh* demonstrator can only be revealed to you by the Spirit, not by man.

Money Cometh is not a slogan; it is supernatural language sent from Heaven. And anything sent from Heaven must operate by the Spirit.

GOING beyond the flesh includes going beyond the strategies of the world. What happens when Christians rely too heavily on budgets and vision boards? They end up trying to *make* divine prosperity come to pass in their lives without God. The ultimate problem with man-made strategies is that they can block supernatural money. They can cause you to forget the bigger picture set by God, and suddenly it becomes about your money and not about God's money.

The revelation of *Money Cometh* is not designed for the secular world, which means demonstrators of it cannot function with money the same way the world does, with paper alone. Instead, we are to make financial moves guided by the Holy Spirit.

When we do this, shocking things happen. A 30-year mortgage can be cut off decades before its time. Financial breakthroughs can happen at any moment, in any way, and with any amount. All limits are shut down.

The world expects you to live under the same terms they do—like being trapped under debt for decades—but you don't have to. God has endless ways to get His children to their wealthy place. His strategies go far beyond the mindset of man. He can move, demonstrate, and deviate however He pleases and through whomever He chooses. But you must be spiritually informed.

The Spirit reveals how far to go or not go and gives discernment when Satan tries to deceive you. Many times, that deception comes through emotion. And emotional moves with money have hindered the Body of Christ for years. They are of the world, not of Heaven—and for a child of God, moves outside of the Spirit are both dangerous and stressful.

Spirit-Led Enlightenment

One of our greatest marks as believers is that God designed us to move in revelation and enlightenment. What enlightenment does is take us beyond excitement and bring us into the realm of divine manifestation and demonstration.

For this reason, I continue to emphasize that *Money Cometh* is a spiritual matter on which you must be enlightened. With that enlightenment comes a greater ease with money. Even further, you'll experience financial wisdom from God—wisdom that most in high places, including those in the pulpit, may never understand.

As with all things that are spiritual, *Money Cometh* demonstration must involve Spirit-led guidance and instruction. The Holy Spirit is the only one that can explain how to get *out* of the way and *in* the way to flow supernaturally.

See it this way: *Money Cometh* is pregnant with the same power, authority, and anointing that is also in the gifts of the Spirit. They have the same origin. Just as spiritual gifts are not functional or understood without the overseeing and administration of the Spirit, so is *Money Cometh.*[2] If the Holy Spirit is not involved in unfolding this revelation, you'll miss it.

You cannot afford to waste time considering your educational background, personal agenda, family history, or skin color. Neither should you focus on how long you've dealt with financial struggles, how many hours you've prayed, or how often you've attended church. Those things can only produce demonstrations of flesh and religion, creating faith that stands in the wisdom of men. But we are to function in demonstration of the Spirit and power, producing faith that could only stand in the power of God.

In First Corinthians 2, the Apostle Paul speaks of his own convictions while also giving us a demonstrator blueprint. He addressed the Christians in Corinth:

> "I, brethren, when I came to you,
> came not with excellency of
> speech or of wisdom, declaring
> unto you the testimony of God.
> For I determined not to know any
> thing among you, save [except]
> Jesus Christ, and him crucified.

> And I was with you in weakness, and
> in fear, and in much trembling.
> And my speech and my preaching
> was not with enticing words of
> man's wisdom, but in demonstration of the Spirit and of power:"
>
> — 1 CORINTHIANS 2:1-4

How Paul ends in verse four is the only way to reach the results of verse five:

> "That your faith should not stand in
> the wisdom of men, but in the
> power of God."
>
> — 1 CORINTHIANS 2:5

When we are Spirit-led, we become inspired by the abilities of God and begin demonstrating out-of-the-ordinary manifestations. Children of God are set apart and must move as such, operating beyond man's wisdom.

~

Money Cometh is a misunderstood foundation of life and a newly revealed economy that goes beyond the flesh. Once you fully grab hold of that truth, your reverence for it will follow. With reverence comes respect—and that respect will be rooted in knowing that it is a real, ready, and able word from God that will not return to Him void.[3] It's from that point it will begin to function in your life as it should.

Money Cometh is a misunderstood foundation of life and a newly revealed economy that goes beyond the flesh.

There is no three-step process to becoming a *Money Cometh* demonstrator. It's right now, and it's supernatural. This is why you cannot systemize your finances according to the world's way of doing things—but instead, allow your finances to become spiritual. God doesn't want His children fighting with the system, so He desires to spiritualize their finances.

Without a revelation of *Money Cometh* and its spiritual functions, your financial choices can easily become part of a worldly routine, just another thing you do. But with revelation, everything changes. Every move with your finances becomes a spiritual move.

SEPARATION AND CONNECTION

Separation means removing any weight, thought, or person holding you down or holding you back.

The journey of Abraham didn't start with blessings—it started with separation. God called him to leave everything familiar and trust Him for what was next.

The Lord said to Abram: "Get thee out of thy country, and from thy kindred, and from thy father's house, unto a land that I will shew thee" (Genesis 12:1).

If the principle of this scripture is not fulfilled in your life, it may be the very thing hindering you from becoming a *Money Cometh* demonstrator.

It's necessary to separate yourself and step into the land God has shown you. He's leading you to another level, and that journey requires the right connection *and* the right separation. If you don't make the separation, you can never make the connection.

Separation means removing any weight, thought, or person holding you down or holding you back. You'll have to separate from doubt and unbelief. For many, this also means separating from family and friends, whether they're physically relocating or mentally moving away from their mindsets and opinions. For those dealing with thinking limitations connected to skin color, that must go as well.

If you don't make the separation, you can never make the connection.

As a *Money Cometh* demonstrator, you must also separate from those who speak against prosperity. Don't give them your ears. You'll find religious Christians are among this number—because when you begin walking in revelation, religion becomes crippled. Although they serve the same God, they can't handle it because they've resisted this truth in their lives. Come out from among them and connect with those who *have* received the revelation.

~

SEPARATION WILL OFTEN BE MET with persecution and opposition, but even in the face of this, don't look back. The *Money Cometh* revelation calls you into a new land—the land of the remnant. And now is the time to start landing.

This is a spiritual land, a revelation that must be revealed to you personally by the Holy Spirit. You can't find it on your own without the Spirit, and no one can cause it to work automatically in your life. As we read in Genesis 12:1, God must first "show you", and only then can you move into it.

He will open it up to you—not just through revelation,

not just through anointing, not just through impartation, not just through manifestation—but also through demonstration.

The Money Cometh revelation calls you into a new land—the land of the remnant.

GOD WILL SHOW YOU; then, He will *make* you. We saw "show" in the first verse of Genesis 12, but now, we'll see "make" in the second verse, where God lays out His promises to Abram for his obedience:

> "And I will *make* of thee a great
> nation, and I will bless thee, and
> *make* thy name great; and thou
> shalt be a blessing:"
>
> — GENESIS 12:2

The third verse identifies who will share in the blessing and who will not:

> "And I will bless them that bless thee,
> and curse him that curseth thee:
> and in thee shall all families of
> the earth be blessed."
>
> — GENESIS 12:3

I don't know why ministers and denominations continue to fight the prosperity message. What did God mean by "bless thee" here? In case you thought it meant Abraham was spiritually rich, the Word clearly lists the details:

> "And Abram was very rich in cattle,
> in silver, and in gold."
>
> — GENESIS 13:2

The Lord was not only speaking to Abram but also to the remnant of His children who have decided to become demonstrators. And we must follow suit. He's still declaring today, "I will bless them that bless you, and curse them that curse you, and in you shall all families of the earth be blessed."

God has used me as both an instrument and a demonstrator for the Body of Christ. He spoke to me in the same way that He spoke to Abram, saying, "I will bless you and make your name great, and you shall be a blessing. I will bless them that bless you and curse them that curse you."

I am living this scripture today—it has come to pass exactly as He said. I've gone to the land He showed me, and the blessings have followed.

And here's the good news: He wasn't only speaking to me. The anointing on *Money Cometh* is transferable. In other words, the transfer God made with Abraham is on *Money Cometh*, and the blessing belongs to anyone who makes the firm decision to connect properly.

Just as God said that those who bless me are blessed—that goes for you, too! Those who bless you will be blessed.

Get ready for uncommon financial instruction—instruction that you will have to meditate; instruction that may even make you cry. Enlightenment, insight, and special visitation from Heaven are beyond psychology and technology—and to align with it means not always functioning in the sensible realm. The money coming to you is already in place—many times in unlikely places and unlikely amounts that only the Holy Spirit can help you see.

Become a Decision-Maker

Once, I told a political man that God had specifically chosen him for the position because he would not make choices, he would make decisions. That word from God also fits the personality of a *Money Cometh* demonstrator walking out the principle of separating to connect.

The spiritual realm sets up demonstrators to make divine decisions daily. God doesn't need demonstrators to make choices. He needs them to make decisions—personal ones.

To make a choice is to wonder how the person sitting next to you feels about it. To decide is to laser focus on what God said to do, despite how anyone feels. Choices will have you split and unsure, while decisions will put you in a totally new position with confidence.

As a demonstrator, God doesn't need you to make choices. He needs you to make decisions.

Whenever the Spirit leads you to do something that separates you, move as a decision-maker, functioning from the understanding of John 2:5.

> "...Whatsoever he saith unto you,
> do it."
>
> —JOHN 2:5

To manifest as a demonstrator, your separated walk must be personal, Spirit-led, and *decisive*.

COVENANT OVER COVETING

We don't have to covet money when we have a covenant with the Father.

What if millions of Christians have been held back financially because of one misunderstood verse? This verse has been like a demonic dog barking against finances and running wild through the Church for decades. It lives in the opening of First Timothy 6:10:

> *For the love of money is the root of all evil—*

This Scripture, when misquoted or taken out of context, has kept believers broke and bound to a level beneath what God intended for them. It has tied up God's kingdom business on earth and held the Church in a position that He is not satisfied with. In addition, it has caused God's children to feel guilty and afraid to talk about money.

This misinterpretation has built a mindset of lack and limitation across generations.

Have you ever wondered why money is demonized in normal church settings? Shouldn't being broke and in financial distress be demonized instead?

Money puts food on our tables, clothes on our backs, a roof over our heads, and gives us cars to drive. Beyond that, we take care of God's business with it. Yet today, it's not uncommon to hear a Christian speak as if being broke makes them more spiritual or holier than someone else. They'll say things like, 'I don't want money; I only want Jesus,' while living from paycheck to paycheck, working two jobs, and struggling to make ends meet. In a way, they're in the same boat as those who rely on the world's system for increase, trying to make prosperity happen in their lives without God. That's *evil.* That type of lifestyle is hell on earth, and it was never meant to become the financial cycle of God's children.

Sadly, in error, First Timothy 6:10 has become a financial killer. To deal with it properly, we must read past the opening of the verse and tackle it in its entirety:

> "For the love of money is the root of all evil: which while some coveted after, they have erred from the faith, and pierced themselves through with many sorrows."
>
> — 1 TIMOTHY 6:10

The second part of this verse, which is rarely quoted, reveals that the "some" referred to here are those who "coveted after" money. By definition, to *covet* something means to have inordinate desire or to seek excessively after it, especially what belongs to another. So why have we put the entire Body of Christ in this verse? It clearly states that *some* coveted after money, and then it points out that these particular people have "erred from the faith."

The world fulfills this verse, not the children of God, who have surrendered their hearts to Him and know what it means to be a sower. Coveting money is not how *we* function. We don't have to covet money when we have a covenant with the Father. This flip on understanding is where we discover the power in reversing the pull.

Coveting money is not how we function. We don't have to covet money when we have a covenant with the Father.

Reverse the Pull

Let's bring more clarity to First Timothy 6:10. The *love* of money is evil—that's when you love money more than you love God. To love money is to not be a giver. Loving money keeps money in control of you; but God desires for you to be in control of money—to have dominion over it.

When you have dominion over money, you follow God's instructions concerning finances and give easily without holding back. This is where sowing becomes crucial. What sowing does is teach you to get over money and reverse the pull. Instead of money pulling you in different directions, you put a divine pull on money.

When you operate according to this revelation, you no longer go after money, but money comes after you. (I explore this principle in depth in my book *Never Go After Money*.) This pull reversal takes place when you catch the revelation of *Money Cometh* and understand that all money is to glorify God.

Instead of chasing opportunities, opportunities run you down. Instead of focusing on what you can do to pay your bills, you focus on what God tells you to do, and your bills are paid supernaturally. You become so debt-free that if God tells you to pay off someone else's bills, you are willing and able to do it.

Instead of chasing opportunities, opportunities run you down.

You become a demonstrator of all that God is, all that God has, and all that God can do. You don't depend on the world to rescue you. And the best part? You understand that First Timothy 6:10 was never even about you.

You don't live there; you live in the next verse:

> "But thou, O man of God, flee these things; and follow after righteousness, godliness, faith, love, patience, meekness."
>
> — 1 TIMOTHY 6:11

Does this describe what you're already doing? If so, you —man or woman of God—have fled the idea of loving money and will only follow after righteousness, godliness, faith, love, patience, and meekness. In this position, you walk in what belongs to you, not believing the lies, and you allow God to bless you as much as He desires.

Those who misunderstand the prosperity message believe that when God's children walk in divine places of blessing, they can't continue living a godly lifestyle—but that's not true. I'm here to tell you that you can walk in wealth, prosperity, and more than enough and *still* be holy and sanctified. The problem is that most do not continue reading beyond verse 10.

Later in the same chapter, Apostle Paul adds this instruction:

> "Charge them that are rich in this world, that they be not high-minded, nor trust in uncertain riches, but in the living God, who giveth us richly all things to enjoy."
>
> —1 TIMOTHY 6:17

What is the Apostle Paul clarifying here? First, he's saying that those who are "rich in this world" are not to be high-minded or trust in their riches but to trust in the living God. Second, he makes us aware that God is the One who gives us "richly" all things to enjoy.

Think about the principle and process of seedtime and harvest. Sowing disciplines you to not be high-minded or ignore God when you receive more. It keeps your heart in the right place as wealth increases.

The following two verses read:

> "That they [those who are rich in

this world] do good, that they be
rich in good works, ready to
distribute, willing to
communicate;
Laying up in store for themselves a
good foundation against the time
to come, that they may lay hold
on eternal life."

—1 TIMOTHY 6:18-19

The latter part of this passage — "...that they may lay hold of eternal life"—shows us that rich people are not excluded from eternal life. You don't have to be high-minded when you have lots of money in this world. You can also be *rich in good works*, *ready to distribute*, and *willing to communicate*, as Paul explained. This brings us to the foundation of it all—understanding what covenant wealth is and how it differs from worldly wealth.

Covenant Partnership

"But thou shalt remember
the Lord thy God: for it is he that
giveth thee power to get wealth,
that he may establish his
covenant which he sware unto
thy fathers, as it is this day."

— DEUTERONOMY 8:18

Who can argue with Deuteronomy 8:18? Our Father gives us "power to get wealth" so He may "establish His covenant". Covenant wealth differs from worldly wealth because you are operating in partnership with God.

You are designed to live in this partnership with God and not be enslaved to the world's system. To be clear, their system was designed to live under *you*, not the other way around. As a born-again believer, you walk with the One who owns everything. When we forget that the Word says, "the earth is the Lord's",[1] we forget who we are and whose we are.

God's covenant cannot be established in your life unless you allow Him to fully do what He wants to do. When you depend on the world for financial freedom instead of His covenant promises, you dishonor Him—you deny the One who is the source of everything you need. You walk outside of the covenant reality that belongs to you. You walk as one who does not believe God's partnership in finances is possible.

When you depend on the world for financial freedom instead of His covenant promises, you dishonor Him, and you deny the One who is the source of everything you need.

Living as a wealthy, debt-free *Money Cometh* demonstrator is not only possible—it's easy. With no regard for the world's economy, you function from a different realm altogether. You shift from the mindset of struggling to keep up in a rat race to a mindset that can only think of being prosperous with all financial trust in God. You stop complaining about money and begin commanding money.

Our Father is calling you to a wealthy place, with holiness and sanctification. This is not about relying on a job's salary to cancel debt; this is about understanding that debt cancellation and an overwhelming supply belong to you supernaturally. Believers are to live extraordinary financial lives because it's their divine inheritance.

The demonstration of *Money Cometh* can become real in your life if you let it. It's only a matter of whether you believe it. Ask yourself, *Will I continue operating under the world's financial limitations, or will I finally step into the covenant reality that's already mine?*

Money Cometh is part of God's prophetic plan to reposition His people as they should be. You were never meant to love money, covet money, or be controlled by money. You were designed to reverse the pull and have dominion over money through covenant partnership with the Father.

YOUR OWNERSHIP & STEWARDSHIP ALIGNED

You have a built-in certificate of ownership for living in financial freedom.

If grace had to be defined using one word, it would be *ownership*—what already belongs to us. If faith had to be defined in one word, it would be *stewardship*—how we manage what belongs to us.

For years, religion has tried to make faith (stewardship) take the place of grace (ownership), but it doesn't work that way. Faith cannot replace grace; it must work with grace. We've thought we could do things by faith that only grace *and* faith can do together. The two must be properly mixed at all times.

Faith operates on the foundation of grace because grace tells us, "It's already done." In other words, the grace of God has already put things in place, and faith connects us to those things. What happens is our faith's stewardship serves a subpoena on grace's ownership, calling forth what Heaven has already decreed.

According to grace, you are already rich and living an abundant life on purpose. My assignment as an apostle of Jesus Christ is to bring that revelation back into light, so that your faith, hope, imagination, and conscience can walk in and demonstrate it.

Money Cometh is full of grace and truth, and it must be submitted to *by faith.* That means grace, truth, and faith must all align to walk in God's financial favor and abundance.

God pre-positioned His children to live a blessed life. But do you believe that? If you truly believed what Heaven said was yours, you would stop trying to get faith to do what's already done by grace. And when you think about wealth, increase, and abundance, you wouldn't see them as things you're trying to obtain or pray about. Prayer doesn't activate what you own; faith does that. Yet, most Christians are so busy *asking* in prayer that they never *demand* what's theirs.

If you truly believed what Heaven said was yours, you would stop trying to get faith to do what's already done by grace.

When someone has something that belongs to you; you don't have to pray about it. You take it with no questions asked. Do you pray about picking up your package from the post office? Of course not. Your name and address are on it, so you take it home. This is no different. You decree God's prophetic word and take it because you know it's yours.

When you decree a thing, you are snatching it toward

you. The words *Money Cometh* will snatch your money out of the world's hands, because you are making a demand on what already belongs to you. See all your blessings as past tense. They have already been provided, and you have been given the power to take it.

The world of lies has systematically trained many of God's children to owe, not own. For this reason, in order to live as a *Money Cometh* demonstrator, you must unlearn the ways of the world's system and move into your revealed ownership.

You are not called to a normal lifestyle; you are called to step through supernatural portals that shift everything. There are miracles, signs, and wonders waiting in those portals for your life, but they only open through the spiritual world of truth.

Ephesians 2:8 tells us:

> "For by grace are ye saved through
> faith; and that not of yourselves:
> it is the gift of God."
>
> — EPHESIANS 2:8

This settles everything in your life when you understand the connection between grace and faith. It's a divine way out of any mess or mistake. It's a divine setup that has been hidden from many by the enemy—because he knows that if you ever stop chasing what's already yours, you'll start living in it.

It's a divine setup that has been hidden from many by the enemy—because he knows that

if you ever stop chasing what's already yours, you'll start living in it.

We Are Not Designed to Beg

The majority of money traffic in the world's system tries to ignore the Church. Instead of seeing the Church blessed, they call her broke and beggarly. Many ministers have even trained their members to say begging prayers, but that shouldn't be. It's not what God intended for the Body of Christ.

I believe this is why God has made my church, Word of Life Christian Center, a demonstrator. Our city and the surrounding cities can't see us as beggarly or broke. God has blessed us in a way that can't be ignored.

The enemy wants us to waste hours and hours begging, trying to get what we already have and be who we already are. But as I've continued to impress upon you throughout this book, when you operate in *Money Cometh* you are operating in an anointed taking of the financial freedom that's rightfully yours. If you're begging God to help you with your finances? Stop.

The enemy wants us to waste hours and hours begging, trying to get what we already have and be who we already are.

Take your rightful ownership from the covenant you have with our Father. There should be absolutely no begging. Exchange the word *beg* in your mind with the word *blessed*.

The Power That Works in You

If you're not living in abundance, but abundance has been provided for you, what could be the problem? The answer is ignorance. Through ignorance, the children of God have given it to the enemy. Christians have been on the thief side of abundance far too long. In the book of John, Jesus made this statement:

> "The thief cometh not, but for to steal, and to kill, and to destroy: I am come that they *might* have life, and that they *might* have it more abundantly."
>
> — JOHN 10:10

It's time to move beyond the "might" that Jesus mentions in this verse and begin living on the abundant side. When we read Ephesians 3, we see what causes you to move beyond that *might*:

> "Now unto him that is able to do exceeding abundantly above all that we ask or think, according to the power that worketh in us."
>
> — EPHESIANS 3:20

Who determines your abundant life? Not Satan. Not even God. You do. God moves in your life *according to the power that works in you*—not the power that is working in Jesus or the power working in your pastor. In this verse, God is telling you, "Look, I'm able to go exceeding abundantly above all that you ask or think. But I can't do it unless I have your permission." The only person who can hold back your right to life more abundantly is *you*, because that's where the power works from.

YOUR PARTNERSHIP WITH GOD'S KINGDOM

Kingdom wealth is available for you to receive, but it operates under the principles of seedtime and harvest.

There was a rich young ruler who came running to Jesus. He kneeled and asked, "Good Master, what shall I do that I may inherit eternal life?" Jesus responded, "Why callest thou me good? There is none good but one, that is, God. Thou knowest the commandments, Do not commit adultery, Do not kill, Do not steal, Do not bear false witness, Defraud not, Honour thy father and mother" (Mark 10:17-19).

The young ruler answered: "Master, all these have I observed from my youth." Then, Jesus, beholding him, loved him, and said, "One thing thou lackest: go thy way, sell whatsoever thou hast, and give to the poor, and thou shalt have treasure in heaven: and come, take up the cross, and follow me" (vv. 20—21).

The young ruler wasn't excited to hear that instruction. Actually, his running and kneeling didn't count for anything when it came to the money instructions Jesus gave him.

The story goes on to describe his disappointment:

> "And he was sad at that saying, and went away grieved, for he had great possessions"
>
> — MARK 10:22

He had great possessions, but really, the possessions had him. At that pivotal moment, he couldn't give as Jesus instructed. He had obviously gotten to a place that's beyond his ability to honor God with what he had. The Lord was trying to train him, but since he had no idea of God's ways, he walked away sad.

The Lord was trying to train him, but since he had no idea of God's ways, he walked away sad.

The rich young ruler's failure reveals to us that speaking and kneeling are not enough. Speaking "money cometh" or kneeling to make a request won't change your outcome on its own. There are *Money Cometh* instructions that will come from God that you must follow as well. And within those instructions, you'll always find *giving*. Why? Because while grace is ownership and faith is stewardship, giving is *partnership* with the kingdom of God.

The enemy has done damage to the words "give" and

"sow". For instance, ministers of the gospel have been known to beg for money in the pulpit instead of properly teaching God's people about the prosperity that belongs to them. This happens because they see giving as only an exchange. But giving is not just an exchange, it's an assignment.

Without partnership, grace and faith are misused. If you don't understand that, even as a child of God, you can easily end up in the same position as the rich young ruler—unwilling to partner with God and follow His instructions when it comes to all of your money.

Sowing puts your anchors down. It takes you out of a flip-flop position when God manifests in your life with great prosperity. It firmly plants you where you are called to be.

Giving is partnership with the kingdom of God.

IF YOU'RE NOT in the position of a giver, how can you expect to receive? Even the impartation—divine wisdom and insight—that you are looking to receive from your spiritual leader cannot manifest before your partnership (giving), stewardship (faith), and revelation of ownership (grace). It's impossible to become a demonstrator without this lineup.

If you're not in the position of a giver, how can you expect to receive?

Think about this: do you have a "mouth relationship" with the person God sent to speak into your life or a partnership? In partnership, the connection goes beyond spoken agreements. If we are to function in the kingdom of God, which is a seed kingdom, then everything we do must spring from the principle of seedtime and harvest.

When operating from this truth, come to recognize within yourself that "I can't flow, if I don't sow." To talk about flowing with the kingdom of God but not about becoming a sower violates grace itself. *Money Cometh* is a flow of giving and receiving, and there's no other way you can get into that flow without first being a giver.

Living in a Divine Flow of Supernatural Money & Kingdom Wealth

Our Father does not desire for us to live *normal* financial lives. He desires for us to operate in supernatural money.

To understand what supernatural money looks like, imagine being able to tell someone, "I don't need a payment plan to buy this. Something happened that I can't explain, and now I'm going to pay the whole thing off, today." That's supernatural money at work.

How do you pull the cover off supernatural money in your life? You sow.

Giving creates this type of divine flow—one that our jobs cannot offer. Paychecks are limited to how many hours or the amount of work you've done, but with giving—there's never a limit on what could return in supernatural ways.

Sowing unlocks your abilities to receive from God. Then, supernatural money starts moving and every financial trap that was set moves out of the way. You become a heavy-walking, financial leader in the kingdom of God's agenda on earth. You are not stuck talking about ten thousand dollars all your life. You're unlocked! And you understand that God always has more.

DEMONSTRATORS ARE to walk and live in the mysteries of kingdom wealth. There's no wealth higher than kingdom wealth, because kingdom wealth is about manifestations. It's not just about what you have. It can come through in any amount at any time. You can't measure it. There's no calibration that man has come up with that can keep up with kingdom wealth.

This is vast—much vaster than most Christians are living. May you see that and cooperate with the grace that God has called you to walk in.

Kingdom wealth is available for you to receive, but it operates under the principles of seedtime and harvest. This means it goes beyond the natural ways of trying to "make it happen" by your brain or muscles.

The financial provision of a *Money Cometh* demonstrator isn't limited to physical efforts or intellectual capabilities. Demonstrators have put their finances in God's court, which puts them in the right position as fertile ground to receive instructions from God concerning their finances.

Demonstrators have put their finances in God's court, which puts them in the right

position as fertile ground to receive instructions from God concerning their finances.

Ask yourself: *Are my finances in God's court? Am I in the right position as fertile ground to receive?* If so, you are on the path to unlocking your abilities to receive and becoming a *Money Cometh* demonstrator.

PART II
UNLOCKING YOUR ABILITIES TO RECEIVE

BEING TRAINED TO HANDLE GOD'S WEALTH

If you can manage the seed, you can manage the harvest. But if you can't manage the seed, the harvest is going to manage you.

Prosperity demonstrations are not only about having wealth. It's also about having guidance, direction, insight, and understanding on all financial matters. No matter how much comes in, demonstrators must handle the money—the money must never handle them. They are to be stewards.

Money Cometh demonstrator stewardship defines someone who God's Spirit has trained to handle His wealth, prosperity, abundance, increase, and overflow in the earth's realm, on the kingdom's behalf.

With a cutting edge on what to do and not to do by the Spirit, demonstrators have what would be considered a balanced financial anointing. Because the revelation of *Money Cometh* causes money to come in faster than they can keep up with, their financial moves must be also of the Spirit and *not* of the flesh.[1]

Surrendered Stewardship

When your stewardship is trained in sowing, it becomes surrendered to God. *Surrendered* stewardship is not only the managing of God's prosperity but also understanding that it only belongs to you through grace. If your stewardship is untrained in sowing during your time of receiving, it will be too much for you to handle righteously. When things increase, you're not going to continue walking with God as you should.

How can I say that? Because when you reach the harvest, you're going to have to keep sowing. It doesn't stop. The seed only increases. So, if you didn't sow before, why would you sow after? If you didn't follow God's instructions with your money before, you won't follow his instructions with your money after. This is why training with seed when you have little is so important, because soon much comes rushing in.

If you can manage the seed, you can manage the harvest. But if you can't manage the seed, the harvest is going to manage *you*. For this reason, to become a *Money Cometh* demonstrator, your stewardship must be trained in sowing at the stage you're at now.

In the training stage, God finds out what you can handle. Will you be able to hear his voice even when you're completely out of debt? Will you still show up where God has called you to be, every week, even with no bills at your house? Most people attend church every week because they want God to do something for them. They have no intention of doing anything for God.

At some point, you must answer the question: *Are you a hustler or a steward?* Stewardship training weeds the real you out, determining how much God can allow you to manage. If you're not sowing and tithing now, you won't sow and listen to God for every decision with millions of dollars.

At some point, you must answer the question: Are you a hustler or a steward? Stewardship training weeds the* real *you out.

God is expecting the power of surrendered stewardship to manifest in your life at the level where you are now. Just think: you wake up one day and realize all of your money worries are gone—there's money everywhere; money is chasing you down; money is calling your name so often that you don't have to even think about asking for it; and money is always there when you need it. What would you do next? Most likely something ignorant, if it's not done according to what God is expecting.

The revelation of *Money Cometh* pulls the cover off of supernatural money for the children of God to handle. So, trust me when I say that you don't want seventeen million dollars without the ability and humility to know where and how God says to move. With supernatural money, you want to be in a trained, spiritually balanced position. God wants to promote you, but He doesn't want the promotion to destroy you.

When you surrender something to God, and not to man, you don't have to worry about that thing anymore. Therefore, you'll find great peace, joy, and power in having your stewardship surrendered to Him. He supplies the harvest, overflow, increase, and more than enough for you *and* His work.

Your stewardship cannot increase without your lifestyle increasing—because your stewardship is greater than your lifestyle.

I remember when my lifestyle increased. I had surrendered my stewardship to God, and my life came off the system of natural money, including salaries and other systemic financial avenues. When it did, I was able to see and experience God's supernatural provision.

God is looking for managers of His prosperity, not people who are only focused on their financial agendas. He's looking for people who are:

- able to be trained and developed by Him
- not suspicious of His blessings but are surrendered to His Spirit
- able to hear His instructions on how to live above the world's standard and not depend on the government's system
- willing to totally trust Him to take care of them in all areas

Ask yourself: *Can God talk to me about what to do with what I have? Or am I busy trying to talk to God about what I want to have?*

Above the Noise

To become a *Money Cometh* demonstrator, you must be trained as a spiritual hearer. You must be able to hear above the noise of this world's system and beyond the conversations of religious people. Sowing is a spiritual matter, so you can't be a sower unless you are also a spiritual hearer with ears to hear.

> "But as it is written, Eye hath not seen, nor ear heard, neither have entered into the heart of man, the things which God hath prepared for them that love him. But God hath revealed them unto us by his Spirit: for the Spirit searcheth all things, yea, the deep things of God."
>
> — 1 CORINTHIANS 2:9-10

What ears are you operating from? Hearing naturally and hearing spiritually are two different things. When you begin hearing spiritually concerning your finances, one thing you'll have to stop doing is listening to those who tell you something different.

Once you can hear above the noise, you will begin walking and seeing in the spirit world and no longer allow the secular world to influence or intimidate you because of what you've decided to do and speak.

This is a principle. You can't be a sower until you're first a hearer.

Spiritually Balanced

Seed training is the spiritual balancing that God put in place ahead of time for humankind. He trains us with the seed because He can't train us with the harvest. The harvest comes plenteous and in overflow. If you're not trained to sow before the harvest arrives, you're going to mess up the entire divine flow that He intended for you to live within.

Seed training is the spiritual balancing that God put in place ahead of time for humankind.

Remember that stewardship is supernaturally managing what God's given you, by the Spirit of God. Your stewardship, or management, determines your outcome. Satan and this world's system can't determine your outcome if you don't allow them.

This is about you and God.

There's a divine stewardship anointing that rests upon all *Money Cometh* demonstrators. It's an anointing that shows you how to handle what you have now. With it, demonstrators know that all they have is under God's command.

They hear, see, and understand the mysteries of stewarding the seed and the supernatural harvest.

If you're trying to hold on to something or plan for the future—the secret is to give it over to God's instruction. Don't give in to your natural desires to make your own moves and plans with money. Even every blessing must be turned over to Him. *Everything* belongs to Him.

Despite how you feel about what you possess, nothing

you have is your own. There's nothing you can give that God didn't first give to you. And in the natural realm, anything can fail at any time; but not with God.

> "But Jesus beheld them, and said unto them, With men this is impossible; but with God all things are possible."
>
> — MATTHEW 19:26

Trust in Him and His way of doing things over everything else.

There's nothing you can give that God didn't first give to you.

Any time the Holy Spirit trains someone, He's trying to get that person somewhere else—somewhere better. He calls on them to sow not only to increase their stewardship but also to increase their lifestyle. The stewardship of the seed is training for the stewardship of the harvest.

You're designed to handle God's wealth, prosperity, abundance, increase, and overflow, on the kingdom's behalf. You already have what it takes. Therefore, let the Holy Spirit lead and train you in this area, as He's come to do in every other area in your life.[2]

FOLLOWING AFTER GOD'S INSTRUCTIONS

The grace of Money Cometh will remove all financial disgrace in the family of God by obedience. Your plans must become the plans God has for you.

I've pushed the importance of following divine instruction throughout this book because it's one of the main distinctions that a *Money Cometh* demonstrator wears. They live *inside* of God's financial plans, and He continues to bless them.

If you asked me what a *Money Cometh* demonstrator looked like, I'd say this person looks like *Deuteronomy 28*—someone who follows God's divine order and instruction.

Divine instructions are qualified to position you in the spirit realm to function beyond the limitations of a normal person. The instructions of God often sound abnormal in the natural realm, but along with them come illumination, direction, wisdom, insight, enlightenment, and light. If you believe God enough to follow them, they will move you from operating on the outside to operating from the inside.

Can you imagine being *inside* of God's financial plans and wearing this kind of divine distinction? I wear this distinction. It's because of divine instruction that I live inside the promises of Deuteronomy 28 every day.

> "And it shall come to pass, if thou shalt hearken diligently unto the voice of the Lord thy God, to observe and to do all his commandments which I command thee this day, that the Lord thy God will set thee on high above all nations of the earth.
>
> And all these blessings shall come on thee, and overtake thee, if thou shalt hearken unto the voice of the LORD thy God."
>
> — DEUTERONOMY 28:1-2

This lifestyle—where blessings *overtake thee*—begins with instruction. When you recognize that *Money Cometh* is not just a nice phrase coined by a man, but a revelation from the Holy Ghost, it changes how you hear and follow God's instructions concerning your finances.

Deuteronomy 28 goes on to declare:

> "The LORD shall command the blessing upon thee in thy store-

houses, and in all that thou settest thine hand unto; and he shall bless thee in the land which the LORD thy God giveth thee.

The LORD shall establish thee an holy people unto himself, as he hath sworn unto thee, if thou shalt keep the commandments of the LORD thy God, and walk in his ways.

And all people of the earth shall see that thou art called by the name of the LORD; and they shall be afraid of thee.

And the LORD shall make thee plenteous in goods, in the fruit of thy body, and in the fruit of thy cattle, and in the fruit of thy ground, in the land which the LORD sware unto thy fathers to give thee.

The LORD shall open unto thee his good treasure, the heaven to give the rain unto thy land in his season, and to bless all the work of thine hand: and thou shalt lend unto many nations, and thou shalt not borrow."

— DEUTERONOMY 28:8-12

We cannot ignore the evidence found in Scripture that proves God *wants* to bless His children. He wants to see rich children, rich churches, and rich ministers in the earth's realm. In the verses above, we see where the Church has not aligned with what God desires.

One area is revealed in verse 12: "…and thou shalt lend unto many nations, and thou shalt not borrow." The Church has no concept of that. We've bought into the world's borrowing system—not recognizing what God actually intended for us to have. You are designed to be a lender.

When you *hearken* to God's Word, He positions you to *lend and not borrow*. He never designed you to be *dependent* on borrowing because you are already blessed. All that He has is already yours.[1] As His child, you're meant to manifest abundance, walk in overflow, and become a lender to many.

When you hearken to God's Word, He positions you to lend and not borrow.

What Deuteronomy 28 does is show us how God responds when we diligently obey what He says. The *Money Cometh* gates swing open! God will bless you so richly, you won't be able to keep up with it. I know this is true because I live it.

My life is a testament of Deuteronomy 28. For instance, our ministry owns hundreds of acres of land. We received a divine opportunity to buy it at a time I wasn't seeking land at all. God did that so I can deliver this message to you as a demonstrator with demonstration. That's how He operates.

What am I showing you with this one example? First, you can live in the blessing traffic—which is the goodness and prosperity of our Father—that you're reading about in Deuteronomy; it belongs to you. Second, *Money Cometh* is not about how much your salary can afford. It's about your divine sonship.

When you obey God and follow His plan, step-by-step, millions are easy. God will never let you out give him.

Stop trying to make a living and live the life your Father has already provided for you. There are things He wants to bless you with that you aren't even looking for.

Operating By What God Wants

Move from operating by what you want to operating by what God wants. Demonstrators are guided and provided for by the Lord because they are not caught up in putting their wants before God's wants.

King David, in Psalm 23, describes this type of characteristic that aligns with walking as a *Money Cometh* demonstrator:

> "The LORD is my shepherd; I shall not want"
> He maketh me to lie down in green pastures: he leadeth me beside the still waters. He restoreth my soul: he leadeth me in the paths of righteousness for his name's sake"
>
> — PSALM 23:1-2

The Lord is constantly restoring the soul of a demonstrator, so that he or she can continue walking in divine prosperity. Then, He leads them in the paths of righteousness for His name's sake.

Let's continue:

> "Yea, though I walk through the
> valley of the shadow of death, I
> will fear no evil: for thou art with
> me; thy rod and thy staff they
> comfort me;
> Thou preparest a table before me in
> the presence of mine enemies:
> thou anointest my head with oil;
> my cup runneth over.
> Surely goodness and mercy shall
> follow me all the days of my life:
> and I will dwell in the house of
> the LORD for ever"
>
> — PSALM 23:4-6

A demonstrator's cup runs over. Surely goodness and mercy will follow them all the days of their lives. Psalm 23 demonstrates the blessing traffic and gives evidence of the *Money Cometh* demonstration that should be real for every child of God. When demonstrators walk in blessing traffic, they're dressed in:

- no *want* because God provides and supplies
- a restored soul
- a path of righteousness for the Father's sake
- an anointed head

- a cup that runs over
- goodness and mercy, every day and all day.

This belongs to you! The revelation of *Money Cometh* is about fully yielding to God's plan.[2] The kingdom's plan, purpose, and production of the gospel in the earth's realm happens *through* you, both spiritually and financially. But your plans must become the plans God has for you.

Seedtime and harvest are not only about manifesting the things or outcomes you *want* in life. It's also about manifesting what God wants done through the kingdom and for the gospel overall.

The kingdom's plan, purpose, and production of the gospel in the earth's realm happens through you, both spiritually and financially.

Having the Holy Spirit's Insight on Your Finances

Money Cometh demonstrators walk, see, and hear in the Spirit world and give no place for the secular world to influence or intimidate them. Let's read through Jesus' explanation of being guided by the Holy Spirit in John 16:

> "Howbeit when he, the Spirit of
> truth, is come, he will guide you
> into all truth: for he shall not
> speak of himself; but whatsoever
> he shall hear, that shall he speak:

and he will shew you things to come.
He shall glorify me: for he shall receive of mine, and shall shew it unto you.
All things that the Father hath are mine: therefore said I, that he shall take of mine, and shall shew it unto you."

— JOHN 16:13-15

Religious believers refuse to equate these particular words of Christ to prosperity, wealth, increase, and abundance. They fail to recognize that hearing the divine instructions of the Holy Spirit is important in *every* area of our lives, including finances. The Holy Spirit can unfold financial insight to you, revealing what to do and what *not* to do with the money you are stewarding.

Flesh-led believers, who don't understand the *Money Cometh* revelation, will go as far as attacking your Christianity for recognizing this. But it was never designed for them to access.

It belongs to a remnant of Spirit-led believers who rightfully divide the Word of God and do not walk on religious grounds with this topic. For them, being a demonstrator is an assignment from God, no matter what anyone else says about it.

Jesus & Uncommon Instructions

Allow Jesus Christ, the master demonstrator, to reveal to you the power of operating from uncommon instructions.

When the sixth chapter of John opens, Jesus is being followed by a great multitude—a crowd drawn by the miracles He had done on those who were sick. Jesus went up on a mountain to sit with His disciples, but when He looked up, He noticed a large crowd coming toward Him. He turned to Philip and asked:

> "...Whence shall we buy bread, that
> these may eat?"
>
> — JOHN 6:5

This question was not rooted in fear or lack. Jesus was giving Philip a chance to prove himself. He, on the other hand, already knew what He would do. The next verses reveal Philip's limited thoughts on the situation:

> "And this he said to prove him: for
> he himself knew what he
> would do.
> Philip answered him, Two hundred
> pennyworth of bread is not sufficient for them, that every one of
> them may take a little."
>
> — JOHN 6:6-7

A penny was a Roman denarius. One denarius was a day's wage for common laborers during that time. What Philip was pointing out when he said "two hundred pennyworth" was that even if they had as much as 200 days' worth of wages, they wouldn't have enough to give each person in the crowd even a little. That's just how large the crowd was and how naturally impossible it seemed to Philip to consider having enough to feed them.

Let's continue:

> "One of his disciples, Andrew, Simon Peter's brother, saith unto him [Jesus],
> There is a lad here, which hath five barley loaves, and two small fishes: but what are they among so many?
> And Jesus said, Make the men sit down. Now there was much grass in the place. So the men sat down, in number about five thousand."
>
> — JOHN 6:8-10

Jesus saw the seed—five barley loaves and two small fishes—and knew He was ready to sit the men down. *He knew what He would do!*

> "And Jesus took the loaves; and when he had given thanks, he distributed to the disciples, and the disciples to them that were set down; and likewise of the fishes as much as they would.
> When they were filled, he said unto his disciples, Gather up the fragments that remain, that nothing be lost."

—JOHN 6:11-12

This teaches us two things: A demonstrator never freezes during money issues; they know exactly what to do. And no matter how much you're starting with, sow with thanksgiving, because when uncommon instructions come through God, the results will always be more than enough.

No matter how much you're starting with, sow with thanksgiving, because when uncommon instructions come through God, the results will always be more than enough.

WE SEE Jesus do it again in Matthew 17. A tax issue came up, and He knew the money was already in place. It starts in verse 24:

> "And when they were come to Capernaum, they that received tribute money came to Peter, and said, Doth not your master pay tribute?" (A tribute here represents a mandatory tax.)
>
> He saith, Yes. And when he was come into the house, Jesus prevented him, saying, What thinkest thou, Simon? of whom do the kings of the earth take

> custom or tribute? of their own
> children, or of strangers?
> Peter saith unto him, Of strangers.
> Jesus saith unto him, Then are
> the children free."
>
> — MATTHEW 17:24-26

Before reading further, take a step back. If you glance back to Matthew 16, you'll see that Peter had just received a revelation of Christ[3]. He was positioned for the instructions Jesus gave next:

> "Notwithstanding, lest we should
> offend them, go thou to the sea,
> and cast an hook, and take up
> the fish that first cometh up; and
> when thou hast opened his
> mouth, thou shalt find a piece of
> money: that take, and give unto
> them for me and thee."
>
> — MATTHEW 17:27

This verse reveals a debt-cancellation transaction. And it came with instructions that made no sense at all. Let's break this verse down into the sevenfold instructions Jesus gave:

1. *Go thou to the sea*
2. *Cast a hook*
3. *Take up the fish that first cometh up*
4. *When thou hast opened his mouth*

5. *Thou shalt find a piece of money*
6. *That take*
7. *Give unto them for me and thee*

What happened when Peter followed these abnormal instructions? The money was where Jesus said it would be, in the fish's mouth. God's instructions are not conducive to your senses. If Peter would've relied on the sense realm, it would have robbed him of his solution. The same is true for you and me—the sense realm will rob our solutions.

Everyone will have different instructions, but regardless of what they are, we must operate by faith and walk *by the Spirit.* Divine pathways cannot be calculated; they can only be celebrated. You serve the One who can move anything on your behalf, if you stay connected.

Divine pathways cannot be calculated; they can only be celebrated.

THE DYNAMICS of the Word of God can lead you to places where money is and that the average person knows nothing about. *Money Cometh* is not a guessing game; the money will be where Jesus says it is. Although you don't know where your debt-cancellation is, God knows. He knows when to do it and how to do it. With your cooperation, no one can stop it. He will give you a revelation and make it real to *you* so that no one can talk you out of it.

We're talking about prophetic debt-cancellation. It's not going to be your job, salary, or overtime that does it. It'll be your wisdom, instruction, and obedience. You'll have dreams and visions, and doors will open supernaturally for you.

Think about this: being in debt means Jesus is in debt with you. You're wearing His name and His power on earth, so He wants you to get out. In other words, He's saying, "Let me out! Let me fix it so *we* can get out." Notice: He told Peter to take the money and give it to the collectors for *both* of them. "Me and thee."

Your debt cancellation is not just about you. Jesus wants you out more than you want to get out. However, it's up to you to catch the revelation that you're supposed to be out.

The Lord knows where you are. He knows where you come from. He knows how you were robbed. He knows it's time for your revival and resurrection in finances. But it comes through revelation. Therefore, be receptive. Recognize, "I haven't been here before." It's a path you haven't seen that God wants to take you down.

The Lord knows where you are. He knows where you come from and how you were robbed. He knows it's time for your revival and resurrection in finances.

Money in a fish's mouth is the most unlikely bank that ever existed. Jesus turned a fish's mouth into a bank. The demonstrations you go through financially will not be explainable. How did Jesus know how much money was going to be in the fish's mouth? Do you think He knows how much you need and when you need it? Yes, of course, and He wants to give it to you with instructions from Heaven.

God is pleased to have you, someone who is connected to Him, demonstrate great financially. When the world asks where your wealth came from, you will proudly proclaim you are connected to Him and that His instructions have guided you financially.

TRUSTING GOD DESPITE THE CONDITIONS

When we are Spirit-led, we become inspired by the abilities of God and begin demonstrating out-of-the-ordinary manifestations.

God wants you rich, regardless of the conditions around you. And this is not a new idea. God has had rich children rise in unfavorable circumstances since biblical times.

Take the story of Isaac for example. He was sent away from the city of Gerar after he began demonstrating great power and wealth. The wealth that came to him in that place was a result of listening to God's guidance and sowing during a time of famine in that city.

His story can be a lesson for many in the Body of Christ today who are not living in an overflow of abundance. Because if you are not living in abundance, you are living in a land of famine.

A famine is described as an extreme shortage of crops in a land. What does that look like? Even what most would consider a good salary is actually an extreme shortage in manifestation compared to the overflowing prosperity God has in store. There's an *extreme* difference between God's wealthy place and your regular expected paycheck.

Now, what should you do in a famine? Should you panic? No, you must do as Isaac did during a famine—follow God's instructions with your seed and operate in faith. As Isaac traveled through Gerar's famine land, God spoke:

> "Sojourn in this land, and I will be with thee, and will bless thee; for unto thee, and unto thy seed, I will give all these countries, and I will perform the oath which I sware unto Abraham thy father.
>
> And I will make thy seed to multiply as the stars of heaven, and will give unto thy seed all these countries; and in thy seed shall all the nations of the earth be blessed"
>
> — GENESIS 26:3-4

What God was saying to Isaac was, "Demonstrate." Despite the conditions, God called him to make a move. When Isaac followed through, prosperous results unfolded.

> "Then Isaac sowed in that land, and received in the same year [a] hundredfold: and the Lord blessed him.
>
> And the man waxed great, and went

> forward, and grew until he
> became very great:
> For he had possession of flocks, and
> possession of herds, and great
> store of servants: and the
> Philistines envied him."
>
> — GENESIS 26:12-14

Isaac settled and sowed in that land despite the famine, believing God when He said He'd be with him and bless him. As a lesson to all children of God, we cannot wait for things to get better to sow. God wants to train us through trust and unlock our ability to receive from Him.

It doesn't matter what anyone or any situation says. Trust Him, because He has an idea on how He'll work it out.

IF YOU ARE familiar with the backstory of Isaac, you may wonder why this particular blessing is significant when Isaac was already rich. Well, let's say you have experienced manifestation demonstrations in your life, and a famine-like scenario arises. You would already know what to do to make growth happen!

Demonstrators *have to* demonstrate—it's what they retreat to do first. They don't pretend as if they don't know what to do. They decide and make a move.

Demonstrators have to demonstrate—it's what they retreat to do first.

The significance of the blessing here is that Isaac was already a demonstrator who trusted God and had proof in his life. When God told him to reside there and promised to bless him, Isaac *had to* demonstrate with much faith and sow regardless of the conditions. Because when circumstances suggest things won't work out, a demonstrator still moves forward with God. They recognize the power of a seed, but more importantly, they recognize the power of a seed sown by instruction of the Lord. Isaac didn't respect the conditions; he respected God.

If we keep reading, we'll see God blessed him so greatly that it caused the locals to envy him. The king asked Isaac to go away from them because it was so much.

> "And Abimelech said unto Isaac, Go
> from us; for thou art much
> mightier than we."
>
> — GENESIS 26:16

Instead of saying, "Go from us," they should have asked, "What did you do?" Expressing and manifesting the will of God is embarrassing to those who don't, especially for religious people and family members who've never seen wealth before. This verse also teaches us that someone who can't handle your increase may end up cutting you off.

Money Cometh demonstrators do not personally experience famines. They are divine examples during the famines happening around them. Their days of famine and lack are over because they know what to do to never fall into that again.

Money Cometh demonstrators do not personally experience famines. They are divine examples during the famines happening around them.

A *Money Cometh* demonstrator has spiritual construction around them. They know how to build wealth in any scenario. They know how to influence money. In fact, money becomes open to what they need and want when they walk through the door. Money listens to every word they speak. It doesn't tell them what to do. They tell money what to do.

God wants you to *demonstrate* like this. He will offer you land to sow in, just as He did with Isaac. Through obedience with a seed, you will demonstrate God's power and goodness, in the midst of people who have no idea what to do.

Even in a famine, God can get anything to you, at any time, from anywhere, through anybody. Isaac knew that, and you must, too. You can't afford to forget it. You must think, talk, pray, praise, worship, and meditate on the Word of God full of that type of confidence in Him.

— Excerpt from my book, *Money Cometh Hidden Wisdom*

SURRENDERING EVERYTHING TO GOD

God owns everything; we own nothing.

The children of God were *never* meant to depend on the world's systems for financial freedom. I've reiterated that in so many ways throughout this book for a reason. Children of God are supposed to depend on God and live above the world's standards and government. It's one thing to know the truth about it, but it's another thing to do it—walking it out requires more of you. In order to live in this life above the world's standard, one must surrender *everything* to God.

There are two ways of surrendering all that you have financially to God: tithing and sowing. To step over the threshold into becoming a sower and tither, an inward decision must be made. While many things may attempt to lock you into a certain financial level, your decision allows the power of Christ, the Holy Spirit, and the Word to bring divine changes in your finances that go beyond the normal traffic of life.

Tithing & Sowing

Tithing and sowing were designed by God as a way for you to get off the system and free yourself from handouts and what the government calls social security. God is asking, "What about your *spiritual* security?" Tithing and sowing are spiritual securities that won't fail.

When you tithe and sow cheerfully, you demonstrate that the system that once controlled you will never control you again. You declare that it won't tell you what you can or can't have any longer.

When you tithe and sow cheerfully, you demonstrate that the system that once controlled you will never control you again.

God wants to put you in charge of *everything*—your income and your outcome. Tithing and sowing will do that! It puts you in charge of everything. Without this in your life, there will consistently be a gap in your financial blessings.

You're simply not wise if you're not a tither and if you're not always looking for another place to sow a seed. Choosing to become a tither and sower will take you off that system and remove the limits the world tries to put on your life.

Tithing and sowing are two personal revelations you must receive for yourself. It's about much more than giving. The power lies in *why* you're giving and *to whom* you're giving.

God's Storehouse

In chapter three of Malachi, God challenged the Israelites to prove Him by upholding their part of the covenant, which included bringing tithes and offerings to the storehouse:

> "Will a man rob God? Yet ye have robbed me. But ye say, Wherein have we robbed thee? In tithes and offerings.
> Ye are cursed with a curse: for ye have robbed me, even this whole nation.
> Bring ye all the tithes into the storehouse, that there may be meat in *mine* house—."
>
> — MALACHI 3:8-10 (PART A)

God then promises that if they give, *He* will pour out a blessing on them. The second part of the verse continues with:

> "—prove me now herewith, saith the Lord of hosts, if I will not open you the windows of heaven, and pour you out a blessing, that there shall not be room enough to receive it."
>
> — MALACHI 3:10 (PART B)

Notice that it's God who is promising to pour out a blessing—not your pastor or spiritual leader. When you tithe, you are not giving to the man or woman of God in the pulpit—you're tithing to God's storehouse. And if you sow directly to your spiritual leader, it's only because God led you to sow that seed into that soil. But your leader doesn't owe you a returned blessing. Your leader won't "open the windows of Heaven and pour you out a blessing so large that there won't be room to receive it." That's God's part! Tithing and sowing are part of the conversations and covenant walk you're having with God.

I'll make this known *again*: sowing unlocks all your abilities to receive from God.

To be a *Money Cometh* demonstrator is to be a giver; they are inseparable. There's no such thing as a demonstrator who is not also a tither and sower.

There's no such thing as a demonstrator who is not also a tither and sower.

Be Free to Give

God's plan has always been for you to be in the position of giving big *and* receiving big in life. But the religious Church has messed up God's plan by taking it into their own hands to force people to give to them.

In pulpits all over the world, begging preachers have crippled the divine prosperity flow that was intended to start through tithing and sowing for the Body of Christ. The conversations around using positive decrees or longer prayer times to spark this flow are backward. Those things should only be to prepare you to become a giver.

Giving is the only thing that sparks the divine prosperity flow in your life. And the *Money Cometh* revelation puts you in position for that flow, where you'll not only remain a big giver, but you'll also remain a big receiver.

Giving is the only thing that sparks the divine prosperity flow in your life.

Fear tactics are used in pulpits to purposely hold Christians down and back. Some pastors have gone as far as embarrassing their members in hopes of forcing them to give. Some spiritual leaders have even lied about what was given as another way to force the congregation's hand.

One tactic I've witnessed ministers use is telling people they'd go to Hell if they don't give. No part of that is true. You won't go to Hell—but what I will say is that choosing not to tithe or sow is unwise because you'll end up experiencing hell on earth if you don't.

When you don't tithe or sow as God leads, you put yourself in a position of relying on this world's system to be your source and not God.

When you don't tithe or sow as God leads, you put yourself in a position of relying on this world's system to be your source and not God.

There's no need to use fear tactics or lies to twist the arms of God's people to give. Sharing the truth about giving, tithing, and the kingdom of God is enough.

When you finally recognize beggars and thieves in pulpits, there is no excuse to be stolen from again. You should be free to step into what God reveals to you personally and follow the instructions He plants in your heart through meditation.[1]

Pondering on the Word of God until the Holy Spirit speaks to you is so important because that divine planting in your heart will carry you in demonstrating, regardless of the games or wrong intentions of anyone. When the Spirit of God comes, He'll find you ready to go.

Being free to give as the Holy Spirit leads will set you free financially. That's my story—that's how I became financially free. I never got stuck in the hype of giving to preachers who were asking for something. I gave freely as the Spirit led me to give.

The surrendered mindset of a *Money Cometh* demonstrator that you must take on is that when you sow, it is not unto a man; you're sowing unto God by instruction. And no one should have their hands in your pocket, forcing you to give. It should only be God with His hands on your heart, trying to get you to another level.

Surrender Your Ways

Are you fully surrendering all to God, including your ways? If you're not handling supernatural money yet, you may have never considered your ways as the stumbling block. There's likely an area beneath your ways of doing things that has been blocking you from receiving from God.

Repeating decrees about what belongs to you will not

be beneficial if you are not first changed from the inside, by a word from God. Instead of arguing with your beliefs, assuming you're doing everything by the will of God, listen to the Holy Spirit. Let Him help you find the holes in your financial bag.

In Haggai, the word of the Lord came through the prophet and spoke:

> "Now therefore thus saith the Lord
> of hosts; Consider your ways.
> Ye have sown much, and bring in
> little; ye eat, but ye have not
> enough; ye drink, but ye are not
> filled with drink; ye clothe you,
> but there is none warm; and he
> that earneth wages earneth
> wages to put it into a bag with
> holes.
> Thus saith the Lord of hosts;
> Consider your ways."
>
> — HAGGAI 1: 5—7

Take an inventory of your life and consider your ways. Once you locate what the enemy is using, you can stop him. You're more powerful than he is, and you have more than enough grace. It's already settled, signed, sealed, and ready to be delivered—but remember that grace (*ownership*) can't work without faith (*stewardship*). We have to steward our finances by faith to activate the grace that has already been provided for us.

What happens as a result of obeying God in considering your ways? His glory shows up.

People shout about the glory of God and don't know what it is. God's glory is all that He is, all that He has, and all that He can do. That's a representation of *Money Cometh.* God's glory never shows up empty-handed. He always wants to bring something to you—something you couldn't do for yourself.

When you recognize His glory and learn to yield in obedience, God will constantly drop things off. Let's continue reading and see what the Lord said after they considered their ways and did what He said to do.

> "Yet once, it is a little while, and I
> will shake the heavens, and the
> earth, and the sea, and the dry
> land;
> And I will shake all nations, and the
> desire of all nations shall come:
> and I will fill this house with
> glory, saith the Lord of hosts."
>
> — HAGGAI 2:6-7

Consider your ways and see the results of God's glory unfold in your own life. It's time to come into the open and let the Lord shine through you. It's time for God to shake up your blessing and anointing. He even wants to shake up your neighbors. He's ready to let them know that you're His child, His hand is upon you, and all that He has is yours.

Consider your ways and see the results of God's glory unfold in your own life. It's time

to come into the open and let the Lord shine through you.

As the Scripture says, "It's a little while." This means it won't be long. If He can do it for a nation in the Old Testament, don't you think He can do it for you today?

The Word takes us further in the following verses and also reveals that God's glory is not just smoke. It shows up with prosperity, wealth, and increase that you can use. Let's keep reading what the Lord spoke in Haggai:

> "The silver is mine, and the gold is mine, saith the Lord of hosts.
> The glory of this latter house shall be greater than of the former, saith the Lord of hosts: and in this place will I give peace, saith the Lord of hosts."
>
> — HAGGAI 2: 8-9

Why do we see silver and gold mentioned at all? Because this is a conversation about God's glory. He said the *glory* of the latter house shall be greater, and the silver and gold are included. Again, I want to stress that the glory is not just smoke. You can't spend "smoke". When you fully surrender to God, including considering your ways in all things, the glory will show up with real wealth that you can spend.

UNDERSTANDING HOW GOD'S KINGDOM WORKS

To properly function from the kingdom of God that's within you, there must be a revelation of how the seed works.

Jesus stood by the Lake of Gennesaret as the people pressed upon Him to hear the word of God. Taking a glance around, Jesus noticed two ships sitting by the lake, but the fishermen were gone out of them. They were on the shore washing their nets, ending their work for the day.

Jesus walked onto Simon's ship and asked if they would push out a little from the land, where He could sit and teach the people. Simon agreed.[1]

For the fishermen, it had been a bad day for business. They'd toiled all night and caught nothing—and no fish meant no sales. Simon, tired from long hours of empty-handed hard work, still agreed to push the ship back as Jesus requested. Simon could have refused, but he made a decision to sow into the Lord.

When Jesus finished speaking to the people, He turned to Simon and said:

> "Launch out into the deep and let
> your nets down for a draught."
>
> — LUKE 5:4

Simon, a well-experienced fisherman, began his response as most of us would in his position, explaining the facts. He answered:

> "Master, we have toiled all night and
> have taken nothing: —"
>
> — LUKE 5:5 (PART A)

Now, what came next in the conversation is shocking. Simon decided not to stop there. He put himself in a mysterious position—a position where God can move, with no regard to the facts. He continued:

> "—nevertheless, at your word, I will
> let down the net."
>
> — LUKE 5:5 (PART B)

Immediately, everything about their circumstances and business changed. Here's what followed:

> "And when they had this done, they
> inclosed a great multitude of
> fishes: and their net brake.

> And they beckoned unto their partners, which were in the other ship, that they should come and help them. And they came, and filled both the ships, so that they began to sink.
> When Simon Peter saw it, he fell down at Jesus' knees, saying, Depart from me; for I am a sinful man, O Lord.
> For he was astonished, and all that were with him, at the draught of the fishes which they had taken."
>
> — LUKE 5:6-9

It was the same ship in the same city. Except this time, there were instructions from Christ, and the divine supply started sinking the ship. Simon gave Jesus his ship to use as a *cheerful* giver, which pleased God.

Giving—and doing it cheerfully—gets God's attention. It's a power that many Christians are not living out as they should. If believers are not shouting about giving as much as they are about receiving, they've been deceived by the enemy and fooled into being takers.

If believers are not shouting about giving as much as they are about receiving, they've been deceived by the enemy and fooled into being takers.

God's Kingdom is a Seed Kingdom

In the New Testament, Jesus unfolds the mystery of the kingdom of God through a number of lessons about the seed, the sower, and the soil. One example is found in the fourth chapter of Mark.

Here, He taught by the seaside once again, and as before, the crowd that gathered around Him was so large that He went to sit inside a ship to teach out of. The people, who'd come from different towns sat along the shore to listen. Jesus began with a parable:

> "Hearken; Behold, there went out a sower to sow:
> And it came to pass, as he sowed, some fell by the way side, and the fowls of the air came and devoured it up.
> And some fell on stony ground, where it had not much earth; and immediately it sprang up, because it had no depth of earth:
> But when the sun was up, it was scorched; and because it had no root, it withered away.
> And some fell among thorns, and the thorns grew up, and choked it, and it yielded no fruit.
> And other fell on good ground, and did yield fruit that sprang up and increased; and brought forth, some thirty, and some sixty, and some a hundred.

> And he said unto them, He that hath
> ears to hear, let him hear."
>
> — MARK 4:3-9

When Jesus closed that teaching by saying, "He who has ears to hear, let him hear", what was He making known? You can be listening to (or reading) a parable and still not *hear* what divine truth it's speaking to you.

Parables are earthly stories with heavenly truths. Not everyone who hears them catches hold of the revelations within them. Hearing naturally and hearing spiritually are two different things. Only those who have fixed their hearts on catching hold of divine truth (with the help of the Holy Spirit) can then hear and interpret the parable with spiritual ears. Those with no spiritual interpretation would have left that teaching confused.

Later, when Jesus had gone away from the crowd, His disciples and a few others who were still around asked about this parable. He said to them:

> "...Unto you it is given to know the
> mystery of the kingdom of God:
> but unto them that are without,
> all these things are done in
> parables:
> That seeing they may see, and not
> perceive; and hearing they may
> hear, and not understand; lest at
> any time they should be
> converted, and their sins should
> be forgiven them."

— MARK 4:11-12

Jesus confirms that the children of God *are* given the capacity to know and receive the mystery. He explained to the remnant of the group that the seed represented the Word of God in the parable:

"The sower soweth the word."

— MARK 4:14

What we then learn is that the sower planted the Word seed into various types of ground, each were different levels of hearers.

The stony ground represents those who immediately receive the Word with joy but lack deep roots in themselves. So, when afflictions arise, they are immediately offended.

In a similar way, the thorny ground represents those who hear the Word but allow life's worries, the deceitfulness of riches, and other desires to choke it, making it unfruitful.

However, when the Word is described as being sown on "good ground"—into those who hear it *and* receive it—it brings forth fruit (Mark 4:15-20).[2]

What does this reveal about the kingdom of God? That its mystery is that it works under the principle of seedtime and harvest. The kingdom of God is a "seed kingdom", and to function properly from it, there must be a revelation of how the seed works.

The kingdom of God is a "seed kingdom",

and to function properly from it, there must be a revelation of how the seed works.

This is one of the most powerful revelations you can have as a believer. And the Holy Spirit is the only One who can reveal it to you, because the way of the seed goes beyond natural understanding.

In this Mark 4 parable, when the sower plants God's Word into a receptive heart—just as a seed is sown into fertile ground—it manifests itself and yields a harvest.

Sowing *always* produces divine manifestation.

The key to accessing the grace hidden within a seed is having ears to hear. God cannot manifest in your life unless you truly hear a *rhema* word, which is a specific word spoken by Him to *you*.

The kingdom of God itself is a seed sown by our Father into the earth, allowing us to live beyond natural limitations. The Bible and all the teaching of Jesus are seeds.

If we look closer at the operations of the kingdom, we'll see that we were also saved by a seed.[3] On the cross, Jesus was a seed sown by God. On the third day, when He resurrected, it demonstrates what a seed will do when it goes down into the right ground—it will always come back up. The lesson here is that if you were even saved by a seed, you must also live your life by a seed.

The entire spiritual spectrum, which is *everything* within the kingdom of God, operates on this foundational principle of seedtime and harvest. God intentionally designed seeds to produce a spiritual, divine life in some form when planted.

The entire spiritual spectrum, which is everything within the kingdom of God, operates on this foundational principle of seedtime and harvest.

THE *MONEY COMETH* revelation is a mystery of divine prosperity that demonstrators can access and manifest at any time. When a financial seed is planted in fertile ground, it produces a divine harvest that puts the sower in a position of freedom—a position where the system of the world can no longer dictate how they're going to come out.

When you follow through with a seed that you were instructed and inspired by God to sow—giving it cheerfully and willfully—it multiplies. Think of what we read in John 6, when Jesus supernaturally fed thousands of people. Once the seed of five loaves and two small fish touched His hands, it all grew, and it didn't stop until everyone had their share and more was left over.[4] When you sow a financial seed with God's instruction, it has the same divine results.

Sowing makes God your supplier, not the world.[5] And when He supplies, He covers it all and more. He supplies the activator *and* the motivator; He supplies the seed, the soil, and the sower. There is no shortage or lack. When the seed gets to work, it takes care of business and always yields more than enough.

WALKING IN PROSPERITY GRACE

Be awakened from the productions of the world's system and see your God-given grace of wealth production.

Decades ago, I sat at a table with five millionaires. They all owned big companies, and I didn't. I wasn't anywhere near being a millionaire at that time. But at the end of the meal, a boldness came over me. I heard, "Take the ticket." And when the ticket came out, I grabbed it.

They felt so sorry for me, but I had to take that ticket regardless of how they felt. Anyone in their right mind would have thought I was crazy for taking a ticket at a table with millionaires, but the Lord told me to do it. Today, I am one of those millionaires sitting at the table.

From those early years of understanding the *Money Cometh* revelation, I permitted the Holy Spirit to grace me to be a sower. God continues to provide the seed, and I continue to sow where He tells me to sow.

When you were born again, your finances were born again. In other words, when you became a child of God and no longer functioned as a child of this world's system, your finances should have also converted. They should've begun operating in another realm of revelation instead of staying in the same place.

Sadly, born-again believers have spent thousands of hours praying about their finances, because while engaged in prayer they are still depending on the world's system. They never fully turn their provisions over to God.

What many Christians don't understand is that prayer alone is not the way out of financial distress. Prayer should always lead to obeying God's instructions, which includes obeying what He says to do with your money.

Ask yourself: *Can I hear the voice of God concerning my finances? Or am I like an icicle hanging from a railing? Am I frozen in my ways and stuck in a stubborn position?* If that's the case, you are limiting God and not accessing the possibilities of His prosperity grace.

Accepting & Walking in The Prophetic Prosperity Grace

Money Cometh is the *prophetic* prosperity grace of God in action. When you speak the words *Money Cometh*, you are prophesying over your finances.

Another word for prophetic grace is "prophetic ownership". *Money Cometh* is speaking supernatural prophetic ownership of prosperity, wealth, increase, abundance, and overflow. And you don't have to wait for your prophetic prosperity ownership to manifest. You can simply decide to receive it, because it's yours. Once you accept and set your heart to hear the revelation of *Money Cometh* as a word from

God, it begins to function in your life situations through sowing and reaping.

When walking in *Money Cometh* demonstrator prophetic grace, you *must* be a sower. As I've pressed upon you in earlier chapters—you should understand that there's no way around it. Sowing came with the revelation of *Money Cometh* all those years ago, and it can't be separated.

The first time I preached this revelation and told the story of how I received it, people started getting out of their seats with money folded in their hands. They brought it to the altar without me ever telling them to bring it. They came *on their own*, cheerfully sowing—and after over 30 years, the sowing flow at the altar hasn't stopped. It's freeing people all over the world. When we accept and walk in this prophetic grace, with and for God, we break free.

One of the greatest disgraces on the Body of Christ has to be financial bondage. But what God was doing when He gave us *Money Cometh* was freeing us from this disgrace.

The "money seed" came to free us and knock the devil out of controlling our finances. Demonstrators, like myself, have sowed their way out and no longer live in bondage to what money once said they can or can't do. They live *free* lives, led by the Holy Spirit, that represent God's glory.

While it belongs to all of God's children, the majority of the Church are still being robbed of this prophetic prosperity grace. They're singing and dancing every week, but after that service ends, the question they must all go back to is this: *Do we represent God in every area of our lives? Do we represent God in our finances, too?*

The "money seed" came to free us and knock the devil out of controlling our finances.

To live the life that God intended, we must no longer limit Him with man-made ways and thoughts concerning money. Children of God are to acknowledge that He is the Father of the seedtime and harvest system and the One who gives them the right to live in financial dominion on His behalf. He is not only a need-supplying God; He is the supplier of the seed, the soil, *and* the sower. And when aligned with His ways and thoughts, that sower, soil, and seed could all be *you*.

Building a Sowing Grace Anointing in Your Life

In the beginning, God established a divine plan where sowing a seed would always come before manifesting a supply. He designed it that way for a reason. When the seed is carried out properly, it carries financial favor from Heaven, which has an endless supply within it that cannot be denied.

Let's look at Second Corinthians 8:7. In this verse, Apostle Paul encouraged church members of Corinth to abound in (or increase in) the grace of giving. He stated:

> "...as ye abound in every thing, in faith, and utterance, and knowledge, and in all diligence, and in your love to us, see that ye abound in this grace also."
>
> — 2 CORINTHIANS 8:7

The grace Apostle Paul is speaking of here is a *sowing grace.*[1] Sowing grace is a grace to cheerfully and freely sow as the Holy Spirit leads you.

I challenge you to develop a prayer life for sowing grace. When you do, you'll gain an obedience that not only supports the gospel but, at the same time, gets you out of the world's financial jungle.

The Church knows very little about having a sowing grace. Yet, it is the sowing grace that sets believers free financially. This grace is not taking anything from you; it's putting you in a position that you'll never have a need or a want. It changes the word *hustling* to the word *holy*. It guides you into living a holy financial life.

~

TO WALK in a sowing grace anointing, first decide to *permit* God to bless you and then *permit* the Holy Spirit to build this in your life. God can only go as far as you permit Him to go.

Sowing grace, sowing anointing, and sowing faith will change your way of living, if you let it. Believe me, the bank of sowing grace is richer than all financial institutions put together!

Tapping into sowing grace shakes you up, but it's worth it. Think of how things were shaken up when I took the ticket at a table with millionaires—but now *I'm* the millionaire.

Those who don't freely sow have allowed money to run their lives. They are in financial turmoil because they haven't permitted the Holy Spirit to build a sowing grace anointing in them. They may think they're holding on to something, but they've allowed money to control them.

What they don't understand is that sowing grace takes their control back. It stops money from controlling their lives and gives them a grace to be in control of money.

What they don't understand is that sowing grace takes their control back. It stops money from controlling their lives and gives them a grace to be in control of money.

See yourself as God sees you, and sow your way out, abounding in this grace. The opposite of that would be to steal from yourself. If you're not open to the voice of the Holy Spirit telling you what to do with the seed that you have in your hand right now, you are robbing yourself.

Grab hold of this revelation in your spirit and soul, and fully endorse it in your life, cheerfully and freely, without anyone twisting your arm. As a result, you'll see manifestations and demonstrations, and you'll walk heavily in a realm and space that is nearly empty in the Body of Christ. God is looking for someone He can flow through and trust in this area.

Knowing this, you cannot afford to be held unconscious anymore. It's time to experience the goodness of God with demonstration in your life. No longer feel at ease with *not* living in divine prosperity and recognize that it's a sin for you not to be blessed. Jesus paid for you to be free in *every* area. So why accept being bound financially? Accept and walk in your prosperity grace, boldly. While Christians around you may still be unconsciously broke and living beneath what God intends, that doesn't have to be you.

Jesus paid for you to be free in every area. So why accept being bound financially?

The truth is that you're not going to sow automatically. God can develop a sowing heart in you and give you strong hands to sow, but you will need grace to do it. You have to allow the Holy Spirit to grace you to sow. It is possible that you haven't fully stepped into that aspect of grace yet, and that's what has been holding back your finances. Maybe not being graced to give is why God hasn't trusted you with much. You ***must*** *have a sowing grace on your life to walk in financial freedom.*

— Excerpt from my book, *Sow & Grow Rich*

BECOMING A WISE SOWER

With all seeds that are affiliated with God comes a resurrection.

The early training grounds of sowing can feel like hanging on a cross. It's painful. There's tremendous pressure involved, and it's completely uncomfortable. But at some point, while on the cross, Jesus said the words, "It is finished." And you will, too.

You'll arrive at a place where your financial struggles will be *finished*. This is called passing the sowing test. You'll get out of financial disgrace through obedience, faith, and grace—and then it's over for good. You financially resurrect, which means your money is no longer in a dying position.

Let's continue from the previous chapter, in Second Corinthians 8, to see how Apostle Paul compares sowing grace to resurrection grace. Starting back at verse 7:

> "Therefore, as ye abound in every

thing, in faith, and utterance, and knowledge, and in all diligence, and in your love to us, see that ye abound in this *grace* also. [*speaking of a sowing grace*]

I speak not by commandment, but by occasion of the forwardness of others, and to prove the sincerity of your love.

For ye know *the grace of our Lord Jesus Christ*, that, though he was rich, yet for your sakes he became poor, that ye through his poverty might be rich."

— 2 CORINTHIANS 8:7-9

Here, Apostle Paul is comparing sowing grace to the resurrection grace of our Lord Jesus Christ. The same Spirit that raised Jesus from the dead is what will raise your seed to cancel all financial distress. The same power that raised Jesus from the dead will raise your seed to break the limitations of your family and take you beyond the level of your last name.

The revelation of sowing is a process that's hidden from the enemy but revealed to God's children. It cannot be seen with natural eyes. From the outside, it looks like something is leaving you, but there's a grace and truth inside of sowing that you must be made aware of from within. Satan doesn't know what you're doing when you sow a seed cheerfully and willingly, just as He didn't know what Jesus was doing on the cross. Jesus was sowing Himself, and Satan had no idea.

The seed reflects the cross because it is redemptive. It redeems you from the law, the system, and Satan's power, and it's full of supernatural security. It runs parallel to the life, death, burial, and resurrection of Jesus Christ.

This means that the harvest that the seed yields is kin to the experience of the resurrection. You must die to the idea of money before money can resurrect in your life. It can't become your idol or god. And you can't hold on to it. You use it—and move as God instructs you.

A FINANCIAL RESURRECTION anointing is on *Money Cometh*, meaning when acted on, it manifests resurrection power in your finances. It brings you where you thought you could never go and gives you access to things your salary says you can't afford.

Are you living on your salary versus turning your salary into seed? Your salary is the seed, not the harvest. You aren't supposed to live off the seed when you're designed to live off the harvest. Your salary doesn't have the ability to bring in everything you've dreamed of. It's nothing compared to what God wants you to have.

This is about no longer having to live by your salary in this natural realm but being able to live by a seed that continuously produces a harvest out of the spirit realm. Therefore, *permit* the Holy Spirit to lead you in what you do with your salary. Your job is a seed producer—it provides seed for you to sow your way off the job. *Permit* the proper use of the seed to take you off the failing financial system of men.

Sowing properly marks you with success that cannot be mocked by this world.

I dare you to turn your salary into seed and see what happens! One morning, you'll walk into the office and tell your boss, "Thank you for the job, but I'm done here." I know it's possible because I did it.

— Excerpt from my book, *Money Cometh Hidden Wisdom*

How to Activate the Power of a Seed

1. Sow when God chooses the soil.

Regardless of where you start, one of the first understandings of a wise sower is that God chooses the soil. A seed sown properly, according to the word God has given you personally, seals the deal for every promise of prosperity, wealth, and abundance written about in the Bible.

You can't just sow anywhere—you must sow in soil that is producing and not in soil that is "seducing". Some people sow under pressure or under psychological principles, not under the Spirit. You must sow as you're led by the Spirit. And God will cause the increase.

> "For the seed shall be prosperous; the
> vine shall give her fruit, and the
> ground shall give her increase,
> and the heavens shall give their
> dew; and I will cause the

> remnant of this people to possess
> all these things."
>
> — ZECHARIAH 8:12

2. Sow cheerfully and consistently.

Start sowing cheerfully and consistently at whatever level you are now, even if you're broke. Why? Because a sower with the right heart cannot stay broke. If you are steady and obedient in this phase, you will be trained to handle whatever God brings next.

Without first being trained to cheerfully *and* consistently give as the Holy Spirit leads, you cannot properly move into the overwhelming supply the Father has prepared for you. Sowing positions you so that when the supply of divine prosperity shows up, it does not take you over.

In Second Corinthians 9, Paul continued to teach a powerful revelation on sowing. He stated:

> "But this I say, He which soweth sparingly shall reap also sparingly; and he which soweth bountifully shall reap also bountifully.
> Every man according as he purposeth in his heart, so let him give; not grudgingly, or of necessity: for God loveth a cheerful giver.
> And God is able to make all grace abound toward you; that ye, always having all sufficiency in all

> things, may abound to every
> good work."
>
> —2 CORINTHIANS 9:6-8

What may be sowing sparingly for one may not be sowing sparingly for another. There are different levels of sowing, but the lesson here is not to be afraid at *any* level. God wants you to be a constant sower, not a contrary sower.

HERE ARE THREE THINGS THAT COULD HOLD YOU BACK FROM CHEERFULLY AND CONSISTENTLY SOWING:

1. Sowing without the counsel of the Holy Spirit. The Holy Spirit must guide you on what to sow.
2. Sowing in fear of bills. Your bills get nervous when you start to sow, because they know they're about to be assassinated. When you sow in faith, you are aligning with God's system.
3. Sowing at the same level. You have to make a level shift, and not just now and then. You must constantly be shifting your sowing level. If you say you're going to sow $200 but the Lord tells you to sow $500, obey Him. You may be stuck at a level sowing that happy, comfortable seed, and the Holy Spirit is trying to tell you to sow something else—something that makes you uncomfortable.

In the early stages of your sowing, your growth moments won't be comfortable, but because you've purposed it in your heart, those moments will be cheerful. When you let cheerfulness overrule the uncomfortableness, you're on your way to becoming a successful, consistent sower.

> "In the morning sow thy seed, and in the evening withhold not thine hand: for thou knowest not whether shall prosper, either this or that, or whether they both shall be alike good."
>
> — ECCLESIASTES 11:6

3. Sow with confidence.

Successful sowers sow with confidence, not fear. What happens is sowing causes your debt to scream that you're going under. The concept of owing the system is satanic, and it doesn't want God's people to get in the vein of sowing. So when you finally break from that system's control and sow, it tries to throw fear at you. A successful sower is someone who has overcome that fear. They have confidence in knowing the process of sowing precious seeds.[1] And they no longer sow like cowards.

Cowardly sowing is when you sow at the same level all the time and don't sow with the counsel of the Holy Spirit —it's sowing as if money is *your* master, not the other way around. However, to sow with confidence, there must come the day where you walk with a purposed heart concerning this.

4. Sow with a purposed heart.

You can only sow what you have, so master *that.* Sowing with a purposed heart makes you money's master for the Master. In Second Kings, we learn what it means to make spiritual, purposed moves with money. Jehoash said to the priests:

> "All the money of the dedicated things that is brought into the house of the Lord, even the money of every one that passeth the account, the money that every man is set at, and all the money that cometh *into any man's heart* to bring into the house of the Lord."
>
> — 2 KINGS 12:4

What does this verse tell us? Don't bring money to the altar or sow any seed if it's not in your heart to give it. If it's not in your heart to do it, you're making a flesh move, not a *spiritual* move.

Sowing with a purposed heart makes you money's master for the Master.

Multiply and Increase

Many of God's people don't believe they can be debt-free by being led by the Spirit, so they try to live off the seed. They're eating the seed. But when you eat the seed, it never gets into the soil and ends up with no harvest. It's the harvest that's going to get you out of debt and sometimes bring in over a hundredfold.

In Second Corinthians 9:10, we learn that God gives seed to the sower. Apostle Paul didn't say God gives seed to the person who owes money to the world's system or who is in need. He said He gives seed to the person who identifies and functions as a *sower*.

In order to be considered a sower, you must be in a *giving* position. He gives seed so that you will not have to owe anyone another day in your life. The verse reads:

> "Now he that ministereth seed to the sower both minister bread for your food, and **multiply** your seed sown, and **increase** the fruits of your righteousness."
>
> — 2 CORINTHIANS 9:10

Two words stand out here: *multiply* and *increase*. This brings us back to the truth that the entire world and spectrum of supernatural manifestation is in the seed. Sowing properly marks you with success that cannot be mocked by this world. God gives you the seed and then feeds you while you're sowing the seed.

> "Give, and it shall be given unto you;

> good measure, pressed down, and
> shaken together, and running
> over, shall men give into your
> bosom. For with the same
> measure that ye mete withal it
> shall be measured to you again."
>
> — LUKE 6:38

God wants you walking freely, giving willingly, and telling this world that it can't hold you down. Once you understand that you don't own anything and everything you have belongs to God, you can flow with Him. And He's going to trust you with more and more.

When we read the story of David giving a fortune from his treasury and challenging others to dedicate their own resources willingly, we see how God wants us to move freely and with joy when we give.

> "Then the chief of the fathers and
> princes of the tribes of Israel and
> the captains of thousands and of
> hundreds, with the rulers of the
> king's work, offered willingly,
> And gave for the service of the house
> of God of gold five thousand
> talents and ten thousand drams,
> and of silver ten thousand
> talents, and of brass eighteen
> thousand talents, and one
> hundred thousand talents of
> iron.
> And they with whom precious stones

> were found gave them to the
> treasure of the house of
> the Lord, by the hand of Jehiel
> the Gershonite.
> Then the people rejoiced, for that
> they offered willingly, because
> with perfect heart they offered
> willingly to the Lord: and David
> the king also rejoiced with great
> joy."
>
> —1 CHRONICLES 29:6-9

Demonstrators can offer so willingly to God because they know they can trust Him. Because they recognize that whatever they have comes from God, He multiplies and gives them more. It's that simple. Demonstrators know He's not going to let them down.

Pass The Test

To become a *Money Cometh* demonstrator, you *must* pass the test, as well as learn and apply these tests understanding the balance of grace, faith, the Word, and wisdom.

The world wants to tell us that we're in a financial mess and then try to convince us to use their system to get out. But those who are in the Body of Christ are not in a financial mess; they are in a financial test.

The tests are there for a reason. The negative tests prepare you for the positive tests. When you're coming out of debt and negative things are hitting you from every angle, it's training you for the positive tests—for the times when you don't have any more negative tests and have money everywhere. You'll be balanced because you trained when you were broke. The seed process would have trained you to trust God. You'll recognize that money doesn't change money; God changes money. Even in a space where God has supplied so much, you'll still consult Him before you do anything and remain humble. If you don't have that training, you'd be stuck-up, going places that you're not supposed to go and trying to show off.

You must pass the test "down here" before you can get "up there". Your training is a divine protection, because money can turn evil if you are not holy. Every test is to get you ready for a blessing.

AFTER YEARS of being trained in sowing, I can say I'm more humble now than I was when I was broke. As we've covered throughout this book, if you don't learn stewardship through sowing, you can easily become high-minded when great wealth arrives. But when you move out of a smaller house into a larger house, you can't stop getting on your knees giving God praise. The word you must replace high-mindedness with is *humbleness*.

I'm so blessed, but the blessing humbles me. Sometimes, I sit on my porch and cry. *How did I get here?* I ask God. I can still remember sitting in front of my old house—it was so small that we didn't have a porch at all. I sat out there in a chair with nothing covering my head, praying to God. Now, you go up six steps to get to my porch, and on the porch, I have two large rocking chairs. I sit there for hours, praying and talking to God.

I'm a man who came from nothing, but God stepped in and unlocked my abilities to receive from Him—and now this man has been sent to help unlock your abilities to receive. It will come to you in the form of revelation first, and then when you act on that revelation, you will demonstrate freely and with joy.

Decree this over your life today:

My abilities to receive from God are unlocked now. It will come in the form of revelation first, and then when I act on that revelation, I will demonstrate. Any kink that Satan has tried to put on me will be fully removed. Any mindset I've gotten from my family or society and anything that has tried to hold me back, won't be able to hold me any longer. I'm coming unlocked today. Revelation and activation are about to overtake my heart and then manifest in my hand.

AFTERWORD

You're not in the same position you were in when you started. Be bold. Many things you've never seen or dreamed of before are about to unfold.

For those reading this, miracle-provoking insights are on the horizon. Many supernatural money miracles are about to manifest in your life.

To step into this, you must be in the proper position and at the level of understanding and anointing necessary. Yield to the Holy Spirit so that He may bring demonstration and power through you. In order to activate the Holy Spirit to bring you to a place you've never been, you must be alert and present.

You are built by God and empowered by His Spirit to walk in places that are not normal. You are designed to experience *money-surprise miracles* consistently. I didn't say salary. I said *money surprises*. The Holy Spirit will show you how to prepare to receive them, because it's your divine right to have them. But to handle these miracles, the Spirit must be in charge. These surprises are too big to see coming through the natural realm. You must be in the spirit.

The miracle world can be a dangerous place if you try to navigate it outside of the Spirit. There are turns you'll have to make—and you'll have to make them just right. When you step into levels too big to maneuver alone, supreme help becomes necessary. This miracle territory you are entering requires spiritual maturity and special guidance to keep you from falling over. It's the only way to function properly on that level and in that depth.

As a child of God, there's revelation, insight, anointing, financial miracles, signs, and wonders available to you. You are a *money-miracle* child. God wants you to expect *money miracles* as you obey what He says. Direction is so important in this area, as well as correction and protection over your finances.

When you yield to God's help, your spiritual life goes to new brackets. Your natural money life ends, and a financial resurrection begins. At that point, you'll never go back to living the same way again.

As you move beyond your natural abilities in finances, always remember this: the money is about the mission; it's not about you. You are *part of* the mission, and God wants you to shine. But the material things of this world are below you, because you are like Him. You are an owner. Remember, grace is ownership and faith is stewardship. That means when you're praying, you're praying out of ownership. And you don't have to pray for what you already own; you make a decision to take it.

Jesus said in John 10:10, "The thief cometh not, but for to steal, and to kill, and to destroy." But that's about to flip.

You're about to take your stuff back. By demonstration of the Spirit and of power, take control.

No longer speak the language of "just enough". Learn to walk in the wisdom of the Spirit within you—the same wisdom that works in your finances. You're going to go places you've never been before and do things you've never done before. You will move without being concerned about how much something costs.

Your broke days are over.

Your "barely getting by" days are over.

Your paycheck-to-paycheck living is over.

Your kingdom supply has no limits!

God is aiming to do more through you, but you must open the valve. Open your understanding and let it flow. Miracles will show up that you didn't pray through; they will come because the Holy Spirit brought them to you. When they do, receive them, believe them, take them, and keep them.

See the included 30-days of *Money Cometh* demonstrator declarations. This special section was created for you to keep close throughout your process of becoming an unshakable *Money Cometh* demonstrator that this world cannot ignore.

30 DAYS OF DEMONSTRATOR DECLARATIONS

DAILY DECREES & READINGS

When you decree a thing, you are snatching it toward you.

TAKING ROOT IN YOUR HEART...

Money Cometh is a success that this world's system cannot change. If the revelation is rooted on the inside, it must manifest on the outside.

MANY CHRISTIANS LIVE NORMAL, POWERLESS LIVES, NOT doing anything out of the ordinary, simply because they have not allowed the Word of God to be planted in their hearts.

Ask yourself: *What has been planted in my heart concerning my finances?*

The principles of *Money Cometh* cannot remain surface-level knowledge; they must be planted to manifest. What has taken root in your being? When the Word of God is planted in your heart, it takes root. It becomes part of who you are, and it cannot be taken away. It is much more grounded than the things your heart has visited or heard. A *planted* Word elevates you from talking about truth to demonstrating it.

Your graduation from "normal listening" of the Word

to "planting" of the Word happens through meditation. Prosperity and good success may already be knocking at your door, but if you're not tuned in to hear it, you won't open the door to access it. Meditation, which takes you beyond normal listening, will train your spiritual ear and align your expectations with Heaven.

To meditate means to soak in the words of God, allowing revelation to take root in your heart. It means spending so much time with what He said that it gets inside you, expands you, and opens you up. You hug the Word and refuse to let it go. Through this soaking in God's thoughts concerning finances, He reveals divine insight and enlightenment that this world cannot stop nor take away. And whenever divine insight shows up, manifestations and demonstrations are waiting to follow.

Imagine how financially smart God could make you? You'll know what decisions to make or not make with money. He desires to do it. He wants His children to be both Spirit-led and financially equipped. The secular world tries to make it seem as though God only wants us on our knees praying—but let me tell you, we can be on our knees and walking in His financial wisdom at the same time.

Experiencing supernatural flows of wealth in this world is not automatic. Only when you settle down and consistently meditate will you expect more than the norm and even rejoice before the manifestation arrives because you're so sure.

Experiencing supernatural flows of wealth in this world is not automatic. Only when you settle down and consistently meditate will you expect more than the norm and even

rejoice before the manifestation arrives because you're so sure.

Joshua 1:8 lays out the principle plainly: meditate day and night, observe to do all that is written, and then you will make your way prosperous and have good success.

> "This book of the law shall not
> depart out of thy mouth; but
> thou shalt meditate therein day
> and night, that thou mayest
> observe to do according to all
> that is written therein: for then
> thou shalt make thy way prosperous, and then thou shalt have
> good success."
>
> — JOSHUA 1:8

If you don't meditate on and plant the revelation of *Money Cometh* in your heart, you won't *observe* it or *do* it. Memorizing or rehearsing the words is not enough. A word from God must take root in you to produce manifestation.

When you meditate, you're giving God permission to change your financial status forever and reveal divine instructions. God cannot go any further than what He's given permission to go. So, I ask: How much of a blessing are you willing to permit God to be in your life?

God has already given you ownership through grace, but your faith must be planted in truth for the two to work together. This means whether you live in the prosperity designed for you is in your hands.

Money Cometh is a success that this world's system cannot

change. If the revelation is rooted on the inside, it *must* manifest on the outside.

Use the following 30 days of *Money Cometh* demonstrator decrees and further study to plant God's perspective in your heart concerning prosperity and your financial situation. Speak the daily *Money Cometh* decrees with confidence, meditate on the scriptures provided, and write down anything the Lord reveals to you. Return to them as often as you need until they take root and change your life forever.

DAY ONE

DECLARE YOUR POWER TO GET WEALTH IS ACTIVATED

SAY ALOUD

I am keeping the power to get wealth activated in my life, at all times.

I am wearing wealth-right consciousness on purpose, glorifying the goodness of God, and keeping the works of God flowing in the earth's realm.

STUDY: DEUTERONOMY 8

> "But thou shalt remember
> the Lord thy God: for it is he that
> giveth thee power to get wealth,
> that he may establish his
> covenant which he sware unto
> thy fathers, as it is this day."
>
> — DEUTERONOMY 8:18

DAY TWO

DECLARE PREVENTION OF WRONG MOVES

Say Aloud

Offers may come that look like what I want but are not what God wants. I will have discernment to see through them. God will prevent me from making the wrong moves with money. To "prevent" means to intervene before an action is taken. Just as Jesus prevented Peter from making the wrong move with money, He will do the same for me.

Study: Matthew 17

> "And when they were come to Capernaum, they that received tribute money came to Peter, and said, Doth not your master pay tribute?
>
> He saith, Yes. And when he was come into the house, Jesus prevented him, saying, What thinkest thou, Simon? of whom do the kings of the earth take custom or tribute? of their own children, or of strangers?"
>
> — MATTHEW 17:24-25

DAY THREE

DECLARE DIVINE REARRANGEMENT

Say Aloud

Every financial change that I need in my life is manifesting right now. It's not by my job or overtime work, but it's by some divine way that God is setting me up. He is rearranging some things just for me.

He has a financial plan to guide me into territories I've never seen before. He has me in a time and area that if I open up there will be a flow in my life.

Study: 2 Chronicles 20

> "When Jehoshaphat and his people came to take away the spoil of them, they found among them in abundance both riches with the dead bodies, and precious jewels, which they stripped off for themselves, more than they could carry away: and they were three days in gathering of the spoil, it was so much."
>
> — 2 CHRONICLES 20:25

DAY FOUR

DECLARE BLESSING TRAFFIC

Say Aloud

Today, I've stepped into blessing traffic because I've decided to follow God's instructions with my finances, at all times.

Blessing traffic is upon me, my house, my family, and my business. Blessings are running me down.

Money demon traffic is anywhere Satan has tricked the Church to live at a low level where God wants to see His glory. Money demon traffic will be stopped against the works of God in my life. I will experience the presence of God's prosperity, abundance, and wealth in my life as God's trusted Money Cometh demonstrator.

In the blessing flow, the financial rat race has to be over in my life. The financial roller coaster I've been on will be shut down in my life. My up and down financial days are over. Money Cometh demonstrations are knocking at my door.

Study: Deuteronomy 28 & Psalm 23

"The LORD shall command the
blessing upon thee in thy storehouses, and in all that thou settest thine hand unto; and he shall bless thee in the land which the LORD thy God giveth thee.
The Lord shall establish thee an holy people unto himself, as he hath sworn unto thee, if thou shalt keep the commandments of the Lord thy God, and walk in his ways.

— DEUTERONOMY 28:8-9

"Yea, though I walk through the valley of the shadow of death, I will fear no evil: for thou art with me; thy rod and thy staff they comfort me; Thou preparest a table before me in the presence of mine enemies: thou anointest my head with oil; my cup runneth over. Surely goodness and mercy shall follow me all the days of my life: and I will dwell in the house of the LORD for ever"

— PSALM 23:4-6

DAY FIVE

DECLARE LIVING BY FINANCIAL REVELATION

Say Aloud

There's a dream team that is about to expose the goodness of God, and I'm on the team! I'm on the team because of revelation in the spirit realm—revelation that I will not try to evaluate or calculate. I'm ready for my financial revelation, today. I turn my finances over to God, because I trust God. From this day forward, I am going to live by financial revelation, and financial revelations will continue to come to me for every area of my life.

Study: 1 Corinthians 2

> "But as it is written, Eye hath not seen, nor ear heard, neither have entered into the heart of man, the things which God hath prepared for them that love him. <u>But God hath revealed them unto us by his Spirit</u>: for the Spirit searcheth all things, yea, the deep things of God."
>
> —1 CORINTHIANS 2:9-10

DAY SIX

DECLARE PROSPERITY OWNERSHIP

Say Aloud

Today, I decide to take ownership of what's mine and walk in what belongs to me, not believing the lies, allowing God to bless me as He pleases.

Whatever belongs to Jesus belongs to me! *It's under a prophetic prosperity grace. As a child of God, I own prosperity, wealth, and debt-free living. From this day forward, I wear the grace of Money Cometh through faith.*

Study: Ephesians 2 & Luke 15

> "For by grace are ye saved through faith; and that not of yourselves: it is the gift of God"
>
> — EPHESIANS 2:8

> "And he said unto him, Son, thou art ever with me, and all that I have is thine."
>
> — LUKE 15:31

DAY SEVEN

DECLARE MONEY INSTRUCTION

SAY ALOUD

Whatever the Holy Spirit knows about money, He will reveal it to me. God will have me in the right place, at the right time, with the right people. A Holy Spirit financial anointing is being released in my life today. Money instruction is upon me. Money instruction is within me. Money instruction is around me, everywhere.

STUDY: JOHN 16

> "Howbeit when he, the Spirit of truth, is come, he will guide you into all truth: for he shall not speak of himself; but whatsoever he shall hear, that shall he speak: and he will shew you things to come. He shall glorify me: for he shall receive of mine, and shall shew it unto you.
>
> All things that the Father hath are mine: therefore said I, that he shall take of mine, and shall shew it unto you."
>
> — JOHN 16:13-15

DAY EIGHT

DECLARE A HOLY FINANCIAL LIFE

Say Aloud

As I yield to the anointing of sowing grace, I will live a holy financial life. The same sowing grace that the people have in Second Corinthians 8 is about to sit on my life.

The insight, anointing, wisdom, grace, and goodness of God are being implanted in my soul and spirit. I will be anointed for wealth and breakthrough—both will come by divine intervention—unstoppable and un-blockable.

Study: 2 Corinthians 8

> "Therefore, as ye abound in every thing, in faith, and utterance, and knowledge, and in all diligence, and in your love to us, see that ye abound in this grace also.
> I speak not by commandment, but by occasion of the forwardness of others, and to prove the sincerity of your love."
>
> — 2 CORINTHIANS 8:7-8

DAY NINE

DECLARE MONEY MIRACLES

Say Aloud

Supernatural money is looking for me—because I'm walking in a financial prosperity anointing. I have a right to be anointed and to have wealth, abundance, and more than enough.

Money Cometh miracles are waiting to flow in my life, and I will get out of the way. I'll never be broke another day in my life. The money just keeps on coming.

Study: John 6

> "And Jesus took the loaves; and when he had given thanks, he distributed to the disciples, and the disciples to them that were set down; and likewise of the fishes as much as they would.
> When they were filled, he said unto his disciples, Gather up the fragments that remain, that nothing be lost."
>
> — JOHN 6:11-12

DAY TEN

DECLARE FINANCIAL RESURRECTION

Say Aloud

Goodbye, lack. I'm not coming back! There will be resurrections in my finances. I'm under an increase, overflow anointing. The rains of blessings are falling. The winds, rivers, and fire of blessings are flowing. And I'm receiving.

The same Spirit that raised Jesus from the dead is what will raise my seed to cancel all financial distress.

Study: 2 Corinthians 8

> "For ye know *the grace of our Lord Jesus Christ*, that, though he was rich, yet for your sakes he became poor, that ye through his poverty might be rich."
>
> — 2 CORINTHIANS 8:9

DAY ELEVEN

DECLARE LENDING DAYS ARE NEAR

Say Aloud

I am designed by God to be the lender. My lending days are nearing. The power is in me, right here, right now. There's about to be explosive changes in my finances on purpose.

When I hearken to God's Word, He positions me to lend and not borrow.

Study: Deuteronomy 28

> "The LORD shall open unto thee his good treasure, the heaven to give the rain unto thy land in his season, and to bless all the work of thine hand: and thou shalt lend unto many nations, and thou shalt not borrow."
>
> — DEUTERONOMY 28:12

DAY TWELVE

DECLARE A SOWING GRACE ANOINTING

Say Aloud

A sowing grace is upon me to cheerfully and freely sow as the Holy Spirit leads me. He gives me the wisdom I need through the sowing process. The Holy Spirit gives me the wisdom I need through the sowing process. Sowing puts me in control of prosperity, abundance, and wealth.

Study: 2 Corinthians 9

> "But this I say, He which soweth sparingly shall reap also sparingly; and he which soweth bountifully shall reap also bountifully.
> Every man according as he purposeth in his heart, so let him give; not grudgingly, or of necessity: for God loveth a cheerful giver.
> And God is able to make all grace abound toward you; that ye, always having all sufficiency in all things, may abound to every good work."
>
> — 2 CORINTHIANS 9:6-8

DAY THIRTEEN

DECLARE MONEY COVENANT OVER COVETING

Say Aloud

I have a covenant with Almighty God about my finances, and because of that I don't have to covet money. I am designed by God to live in His covenant of wealth, and I won't let anyone talk me out of it. They won't say what's so. My Father says what's so. I have fled the idea of loving money and will only follow after righteousness, godliness, faith, love, patience, and meekness. I don't chase what I already own.

Study: 1 Timothy 6

> "For the love of money is the root of all evil: which while some coveted after, they have erred from the faith, and pierced themselves through with many sorrows.
> But thou, O man of God, flee these things; and follow after righteousness, godliness, faith, love, patience, meekness."
>
> — 1 TIMOTHY 6:10-11

DAY FOURTEEN

DECLARE NO FEAR

Say Aloud

I will not fear finances anymore in my life. Financial fright must leave me now.

I shall not need to fight in this battle. Financial salvation is coming to my life today.

Study: 1 Samuel 17

> "And all this assembly shall know that the Lord saveth not with sword and spear: for the battle is the Lord's, and he will give you into our hands."
>
> — 1 SAMUEL 17:47

DAY FIFTEEN

DECLARE FINANCIAL INSIGHT

SAY ALOUD

I will walk in financial insight. The Holy Spirit will tell me what to do and what not to do with money. When it comes down to prosperity, wealth, increase, and abundance; my days of walking in the blind are over. I'm coming unlocked. Kingdom financial business is being assigned to me now.

Every step I take, I expect to be blessed for the rest of my life. I'm not going by feelings, facts, or fear. I'm walking by faith and activating my grace.

STUDY: JOHN 14 & 2 CORINTHIANS 5

> "But the Comforter, which is the Holy Ghost, whom the Father will send in my name, he shall teach you all things, and bring all things to your remembrance, whatsoever I have said unto you."
>
> — JOHN 14:26

> "For we walk by faith, not by sight:"
>
> — 2 CORINTHIANS 5:7

DAY SIXTEEN

DECLARE YOU'RE A SPIRITUAL HEARER

Say Aloud

I am a spiritual hearer. I am able to hear above the noise of this world's system and beyond the conversations of religious people. This means I will begin walking and seeing in the spirit world and no longer allowing the secular world to influence or intimidate me.

Study: 1 Corinthians 2 & Mark 4

> "But as it is written, Eye hath not seen, nor ear heard, neither have entered into the heart of man, the things which God hath prepared for them that love him. But God hath revealed them unto us by his Spirit: for the Spirit searcheth all things, yea, the deep things of God."
>
> — 1 CORINTHIANS 2:9-10

> "And he said unto them, He that hath ears to hear, let him hear."
>
> — MARK 4:9

DAY SEVENTEEN

DECLARE YOU'RE A LIVING SACRIFICE

Say Aloud

I must become a living sacrifice to God. That's the only way I'll ever become a Money Cometh demonstrator!

Maturing in my finances is about being transformed by the renewing of my mind concerning it.

Study: Romans 12

"I beseech you therefore, brethren,
by the mercies of God, that ye
present your bodies a living sacri-
fice, holy, acceptable unto God,
which is your reasonable service.
And be not conformed to this world:
but be ye transformed by the
renewing of your mind, that ye
may prove what is that good, and
acceptable, and perfect, will
of God.

— ROMANS 12:1-2

DAY EIGHTEEN

DECLARE SEALED PROSPERITY & LIFE MORE ABUNDANTLY

Say Aloud

My divine prosperity is sealed; it's not temporary. I will have sealed wealth, sealed abundance, sealed overflow, sealed increase, for the rest of my life.

I walk in the divine provisions of God and live in His divine privileges. The only person who can hold back my right to life more abundantly is me because that's where the power works from. Today I stop blocking the Lord from giving me a life that's more abundant.

It's according to the revelation, insight, understanding, and following of instructions that I can do this.

I can't walk in Money Cometh in a group; I have to make my mind up that I'm hearing from God myself because the power of Money Cometh is in me!

Study: John 10 & Ephesians 3

"The thief cometh not, but for to steal, and to kill, and to destroy: I am come that they might have life, and that they might have it more abundantly."

— JOHN 10:10

"Now unto him that is able to do exceeding abundantly above all that we ask or think, according to the power that worketh in us."

— EPHESIANS 3:20

DAY NINETEEN

DECLARE SUPERNATURAL FINANCIAL RIVERS ARE OPEN

Say Aloud

I am moving in the light and life of 'more than enough'. I have a multiplier and an increaser that is with me at all times. I have no idea what might happen. I am a setup sower.

Supernatural financial rivers are opening. Debt cancellation and supernatural overflow will arise, not only in my life, but throughout the Body of Christ.

Study: 2 Corinthians 9

> "Now he that ministereth seed to the sower both minister bread for your food, and multiply your seed sown, and increase the fruits of your righteousness."
>
> — 2 CORINTHIANS 9:10

DAY TWENTY

DECLARE YOUR WEALTH
A WEAPON FOR GOD

Say Aloud

My wealth is a weapon that God uses. I'm going to let God use His weapon.

I am yielding to money wisdom from God, operating in divine prosperity.

Study: Ecclesiastes 7

> "For wisdom is a defence, and money is a defence: but the excellency of knowledge is, that wisdom giveth life to them that have it."
>
> — ECCLESIASTES 7:12

DAY TWENTY-ONE

DECLARE FINANCIAL HOLES ARE FILLED

Say Aloud

Today, I take inventory of my life and consider my ways. I will see results unfold in my life when I do this.

All financial leaks are leaving my life for good. All financial holes will be filled. God is trying to get insight into me.

Study: Haggai 1

> "Now therefore thus saith
> the Lord of hosts; Consider your ways.
> Ye have sown much, and bring in little; ye eat, but ye have not enough; ye drink, but ye are not filled with drink; ye clothe you, but there is none warm; and he that earneth wages earneth wages to put it into a bag with holes.
> Thus saith the Lord of hosts;
> Consider your ways."
>
> — HAGGAI 1:5-7

DAY TWENTY-TWO

DECLARE FINANCIAL YOKES & BURDENS DESTROYED

Say Aloud

Today, the Holy Spirit anoints me as a Money Cometh demonstrator. My financial status is being supernaturally changed. Financial yokes and burdens are being destroyed right now. I am designed by God to live an over and above lifestyle.

That which was not working for me has gone to work in my favor. All broke strokes are removed and destroyed.

Even my family members can no longer place broke strokes on me. They can try to make it seem like a lifestyle, but it's not my lifestyle anymore!

Study: Isaiah 10 & Genesis 12

> "And it shall come to pass in that day,
> that his burden shall be taken
> away from off thy shoulder, and
> his yoke from off thy neck, and
> the yoke shall be destroyed
> because of the anointing."
>
> — ISAIAH 10:27

"Now the Lord had said unto
Abram, Get thee out of thy
country, and from thy kindred,
and from thy father's house, unto
a land that I will shew thee:
And I will make of thee a great
nation, and I will bless thee, and
make thy name great; and thou
shalt be a blessing:
And I will bless them that bless thee,
and curse him that curseth thee:
and in thee shall all families of
the earth be blessed."

— GENESIS 12:1-3

DAY TWENTY-THREE

DECLARE THE FULLNESS OF YOUR FINANCIAL RIGHTS

SAY ALOUD

I am ready to walk in the fullness of my financial rights.

Because the earth is the Lord's and the fullness thereof God, because I'm walking in the grace of Money Cometh.

STUDY: PSALM 24

> "The earth is the Lord's, and the fulness thereof; the world, and they that dwell therein."
>
> — PSALM 24:1

DAY TWENTY-FOUR

DECLARE EVERYTHING WILL WORK OUT

Say Aloud

Everything will work out. The spirit of happiness is right now. It will work out in my favor. It doesn't matter how bad it looks; it's a done deal. I'm covered right now. My hustling days are over.

Study: Romans 8

> "And we know that all things work
> together for good to them that
> love God, to them who are the
> called according to his purpose."
>
> — ROMANS 8:28

DAY TWENTY-FIVE

DECLARE NO MORE FINANCIAL LIMITS

Say Aloud

At any moment, I can have a money surprise. Let the money miracles flow in my life and in the lives of anyone connected to me. I have no more financial limits.

Where I have been limping financially, I am about to start leaping. Financial freedom is upon me right now.

Study: Luke 1 & Matthew 19

> "For with God nothing shall be impossible."
>
> — LUKE 1:37

> "But Jesus beheld them, and said unto them, With men this is impossible; but with God all things are possible."
>
> — MATTHEW 19:26

DAY TWENTY-SIX

DECLARE AUTHORITY

SAY ALOUD

I have a 'prosperity grace' on me. I have a 'wealth grace' on me. I have an 'abundance grace' on the inside of me. The Lord Jesus Christ is on the inside of me. The Holy Ghost and the kingdom of God is on the inside of me.

Therefore, I have authority. I will not settle for less. My Father has provided for me to have the best!

Money will never control me again. I am a money controller. Money will never decide what I can and can't have. I have authority over money!

Every bit of authority that money had over me is broken, now!

STUDY: LUKE 17

"And when he was demanded of the
Pharisees, when the kingdom of
God should come, he answered
them and said, The kingdom of
God cometh not with
observation:
Neither shall they say, Lo here! or, lo
there! for, behold, the kingdom
of God is within you."

— LUKE 17:20-21

DAY TWENTY-SEVEN

DECLARE MORE AND MORE

Say Aloud

Because I fear God, He will increase me more and more. He's never going to stop. There's a flow of more upon me. I walk and flow in the currents of abundance, freely.

I'm getting ready because more is coming. Levels of increase are on the horizon. My days of "just enough" are over.

Study: Psalm 115

"He will bless them that fear the
Lord, both small and great.
The Lord shall *increase you more and
more, you and your children.*"

— PSALM 115:13-14

DAY TWENTY-EIGHT

DECLARE GOD'S PLEASURE IN YOUR PROSPERITY

SAY ALOUD

My broke-ness makes God sad. My richness makes God glad. In faith, I will take ownership of what's rightfully mine because it pleases God.

I am no longer rehearsing normal patterns—I am reversing them.

STUDY: PSALM 35

> "Let them shout for joy, and be glad,
> that favour my righteous cause:
> yea, let them say continually, Let
> the Lord be magnified, which
> hath pleasure in the prosperity of
> his servant."
>
> — PSALM 35:27

DAY TWENTY-NINE

DECLARE GENERATIONAL WEALTH

SAY ALOUD

Not only will I be wealthy, but my children will be wealthy. The wealth of the sinner will leave the hands of the unjust and be laid up for the hands of God's people.

I'm going to live in God's financial plan for the rest of my life, according to His word.

STUDY: PROVERBS 13

> "A good man leaveth an inheritance to his children's children: and the wealth of the sinner is laid up for the just."
>
> — PROVERBS 13:22

DAY THIRTY

DECLARE THE POWER IN YOU

SAY ALOUD

God moves in my life according to the power that works in me! He is able to go exceeding, abundantly above all that I ask or think.

But He can't do it unless He has my permission. I give Him permission.

STUDY: EPHESIANS 3

> "Now unto him that is able to do exceeding abundantly above all that we ask or think, according to the power that worketh in us."
>
> — EPHESIANS 3:20

NOTES

INTRODUCTION

1. Hosea 4:6. "My people are destroyed for lack of knowledge: because thou hast rejected knowledge, I will also reject thee, that thou shalt be no priest to me: seeing thou hast forgotten the law of thy God, I will also forget thy children."
2. Ephesians 2:19-22. "Now therefore ye are no more strangers and foreigners, but fellowcitizens with the saints, and of the household of God; [20] And are built upon the foundation of the apostles and prophets, Jesus Christ himself being the chief corner stone; [21] In whom all the building fitly framed together groweth unto an holy temple in the Lord: [22] In whom ye also are builded together for an habitation of God through the Spirit."
3. Ephesians 3:5. "Which in other ages was not made known unto the sons of men, as it is now revealed unto his holy apostles and prophets by the Spirit."

1. YOUR DIVINE NATURE OF RICHNESS

1. Psalm 23:4-6. "Yea, though I walk through the valley of the shadow of death, I will fear no evil: for thou art with me; thy rod and thy staff they comfort me; [5] Thou preparest a table before me in the presence of mine enemies: thou anointest my head with oil; my cup runneth over. [6] Surely goodness and mercy shall follow me all the days of my life: and I will dwell in the house of the LORD for ever."

2. BEYOND THE FLESH

1. Isaiah 10:27. "And it shall come to pass in that day, that his burden shall be taken away from off thy shoulder, and his yoke from off thy neck, and the yoke shall be destroyed because of the anointing."
2. Note: In educating us on the spiritual gifts, Apostle Paul is also addressing how all manifestations of the Spirit work in the realm of the supernatural. Regardless of the diversities of gifts that exist, the Spirit is always the same. And with all things that are spiritual, there must be Spirit-led guidance and instruction.

   Reference: 1 Corinthians 12:4-7. "Now there are diversities of gifts, but the same Spirit. [5] And there are differences of administrations, but the same Lord. [6] And there are diversities of operations, but it is the same God which worketh all in all. [7] But the manifestation of the Spirit is given to every man to profit withal."

3. Isaiah 55:11. "So shall my word be that goeth forth out of my mouth: it shall not return unto me void, but it shall accomplish that which I please, and it shall prosper in the thing whereto I sent it."

4. COVENANT OVER COVETING

1. Psalm 24:1. "The earth is the Lord's, and the fulness thereof; the world, and they that dwell therein."

7. BEING TRAINED TO HANDLE GOD'S WEALTH

1. Romans 8:9. "But ye are not in the flesh, but in the Spirit, if so be that the Spirit of God dwell in you. Now if any man have not the Spirit of Christ, he is none of his."
2. John 14:26. "But the Comforter, which is the Holy Ghost, whom the Father will send in my name, he shall teach you all things, and bring all things to your remembrance, whatsoever I have said unto you."

8. FOLLOWING AFTER GOD'S INSTRUCTIONS

1. Luke 15:31. "And he said unto him, Son, thou art ever with me, and all that I have is thine."
2. Jeremiah 29:11. "For I know the thoughts that I think toward you, saith the Lord, thoughts of peace, and not of evil, to give you an expected end."
3. Matthew 16:15-17. "He saith unto them, But whom say ye that I am? [16] And Simon Peter answered and said, Thou art the Christ, the Son of the living God. [17] And Jesus answered and said unto him, Blessed art thou, Simon Barjona: for flesh and blood hath not revealed it unto thee, but my Father which is in heaven."

10. SURRENDERING EVERYTHING TO GOD

1. Joshua 1:8. "This book of the law shall not depart out of thy mouth; but thou shalt meditate therein day and night, that thou mayest

observe to do according to all that is written therein: for then thou shalt make thy way prosperous, and then thou shalt have good success."

11. UNDERSTANDING HOW GOD'S KINGDOM WORKS

1. Luke 5:1-3. "And it came to pass, that, as the people pressed upon him to hear the word of God, he stood by the lake of Gennesaret, [2] And saw two ships standing by the lake: but the fishermen were gone out of them, and were washing their nets. [3] And he entered into one of the ships, which was Simon's, and prayed him that he would thrust out a little from the land. And he sat down, and taught the people out of the ship."
2. Mark 4:15-20. "And these are they by the way side, where the word is sown; but when they have heard, Satan cometh immediately, and taketh away the word that was sown in their hearts. [16] And these are they likewise which are sown on stony ground; who, when they have heard the word, immediately receive it with gladness; [17] And have no root in themselves, and so endure but for a time: afterward, when affliction or persecution ariseth for the word's sake, immediately they are offended. [18] And these are they which are sown among thorns; such as hear the word, [19] And the cares of this world, and the deceitfulness of riches, and the lusts of other things entering in, choke the word, and it becometh unfruitful. [20] And these are they which are sown on good ground; such as hear the word, and receive it, and bring forth fruit, some thirtyfold, some sixty, and some an hundred."
3. John 3:16. "For God so loved the world, that he *gave* his only begotten Son, that whosoever believeth in him should not perish, but have everlasting life."
4. John 6:9-13. "There is a lad here, which hath five barley loaves, and two small fishes: but what are they among so many? [10] And Jesus said, Make the men sit down. Now there was much grass in the place. So the men sat down, in number about five thousand. [11] And Jesus took the loaves; and when he had given thanks, he distributed to the disciples, and the disciples to them that were set down; and likewise of the fishes as much as they would. [12] When they were filled, he said unto his disciples, Gather up the fragments that remain, that nothing be lost. [13] Therefore they gathered them together, and filled twelve baskets with the fragments of the five barley loaves, which remained over and above unto them that had eaten."
5. Philippians 4:19. "But my God shall supply all your need according to his riches in glory by Christ Jesus."

12. WALKING IN PROSPERITY GRACE

1. Reference Second Corinthians 8:1-7 for full context of the sowing grace that was on the people Apostle Paul was describing. "Moreover, brethren, we do you to wit of the grace of God bestowed on the churches of Macedonia; [2] How that in a great trial of affliction the abundance of their joy and their deep poverty abounded unto the riches of their liberality. [3] For to their power, I bear record, yea, and beyond their power they were willing of themselves; [4] Praying us with much intreaty that we would receive the gift, and take upon us the fellowship of the ministering to the saints. [5] And this they did, not as we hoped, but first gave their own selves to the Lord, and unto us by the will of God. [6] Insomuch that we desired Titus, that as he had begun, so he would also finish in you the same grace also. [7] Therefore, as ye abound in every thing, in faith, and utterance, and knowledge, and in all diligence, and in your love to us, see that ye abound in this grace also."

13. BECOMING A WISE SOWER

1. Psalm 126:6: "He that goeth forth and weepeth, bearing precious seed, shall doubtless come again with rejoicing, bringing his sheaves with him."

   This verse reflects how they sowed with confidence because of their maturity in sowing.

ABOUT THE AUTHOR

Louisiana native, Dr. (Apostle) Leroy Thompson Sr. is the Pastor of Word of Life Christian Center and Chief overseer of Leroy Thompson Ministerial Association (LTMA) and Ever Increasing Word Ministries.

With a strong calling from God, Apostle Thompson travels the world taking the message of financial freedom to the Body of Christ by holding *Money Cometh to You* Conferences. He truly believes that God's financial abundance is for every believer. He is the author of several books, including his bestseller "Money Cometh! To The Body of Christ."

Apostle Thompson not only believes but also knows from experience that the key to a successful ministry is the combination of praying in the spirit, living and teaching the Word of Faith, and following after the leadership of the Holy Ghost. He has been happily married to his lovely wife, Mrs. Carolyn A. Thompson, for over 50 years. They have four children—Leroy Jr. (Shantel), Shauna (Jesse), Donavan (Nakia), and Darnell (Deirdre) — who serve full-time in the ministry along with their parents.

instagram.com/drleroysr

facebook.com/ApostleLeroyThompsonSr

tiktok.com/@drleroysr

ALSO BY DR. LEROY THOMPSON, SR.

Money Cometh Hidden Wisdom

Sow & Grow Rich

Money Cometh to the Body of Christ

Never Go After Money

Framing Your World with the Word of God

No More Empty Hands

What To Do When Your Faith Is Challenged

How To Find Your Wealthy Place

Money With A Mission

I'll Never Be Broke Another Day in My Life

Money Thou Art Loosed

You're Not Broke You Have A Seed

BECOME A FINANCIAL FREEDOM PARTNER

with *Ever Increasing Word Ministries*

What does it mean to become a partner? You are in agreement with this vision and this vision is in agreement with you!

Where there is no vision, the people perish: but he that keepeth the law, happy is he.
Proverbs 29:18

PARTNERSHIP PRIVILEGES

- Regular prayer from this ministry for your success and victory
- Monthly impartation and update letter from us
- Monthly MP3 or CD teaching from Apostle Thompson
- An official Financial Freedom Membership Card that enables you to a 20% discount on any products ordered from this ministry
- *Leroy Thompson TV Financial Freedom Partnership Portal*: Gaining access to videos and messages from Apostle Leroy Thompson that are designated for the partners
- Most importantly, you will be exercising the impartation and information you receive to produce a God-fulfilled life!

To become a partner, visit **www.eiwm.org/partnership**, today.